SEO 2018
The New Era of
SEO

INTRODUCTION

As an ever-developing industry, search engine optimization (SEO) has come a very long way. Ever since the industry has been constantly changing, yet, progressing effectively and efficiently as it evolves through the years of our digital age.

SEO has already freed itself from the connotations of mysticisms and trickeries for both of its black and white hat practices in the World Wide Web. Fact is that SEO has now become widely reputed as an essentially indispensable component of any upright digital marketing strategy.

Latest figures speak impressively about business investments in SEO services, reaching more than $60 billion in 2016 alone. Without seeing any causes for a letup in its revenues, the upward trend continues with projections hitting between $70 and $80 billion by the end of 2018.

By the looks of it all, the best and glorious days of SEO are still to come. However, the most difficult aspect in the macrocosm of search is foretelling what actually lies ahead.

Just the same, laying out rational predictions about how the current search engines work and evolve progressively towards the upcoming years can definitely help and benefit us in more ways than we expect them to be.

Foremost, anticipating for any of the likely SEO eventualities in the digital age enables us exercising the prudence of preparing and establishing optimally feasible and desirable strategies about them, even under certain set restrictions, or following, say, Google's suggested practices.

Nevertheless, for us to have a better and more comprehensive understanding of the progressive evolutions of SEO does not mean focusing entirely our anticipations towards a singular aspect or general practice.

After all, you cannot predict how SEO truly works in the future by only concentrating on a single field, like digital marketing. Everything just seems interrelated, so indeed, it takes us digesting actually the whole SEO pie!

Instead, the sensible predictions shall focus across factors that affect each of the variegated SEO details and strategies— attribute renderings (content, latent semantic indexing, etc.), dimensions (domain, keyword, off page, and page levels), property customizations (baiting links, local positioning, etc.), and all other associated fields of SEO.

More importantly, since the principal search engines keep on fine-tuning and updating their search engine results page (SERP) displays and algorithms, SEO professionals must learn to be proactive and refer to previous trend-setting strategies and practices for proper guidance and adapt to imminent changes.

From this standpoint, there looms to be a major troika of design factors and innovations that play key roles, and creates a huge impact on the state of the future of SEO:

💻 **User Experience (UX)**, due to Google's obsession with users, as well as the enhanced customization of search results;

💻 **Accelerated Mobile Pages (AMP)**, due to Google's creation of two indices for drawing search queries— desktop and mobile, with more emphasis upon the latter as primary index; and,

💻 **Artificial Intelligence (AI)**, due to Google's recent installation of the AI-powered RankBrain algorithm system— its third search ranking factor aside from links and contents.

However, since part of this guidebook aims at predicting what lies sooner ahead, you should take these predictions responsibly with a grain of salt. All the points discussed herein are merely thoughtful exercises of confronting and engaging in SEO 2018 practices, regardless of how authoritative this book may be.

Thus, the main objective of this book is presenting you with ideas in light of the latest and predicted search practices with respect to the ever-changing protocols of Search, and thereby, cultivate in you constructive steps or ideal methodologies to take between now and over the next 12 months in the new era of SEO and digital marketing.

As it was in the beginning, today, and towards the new age of SEO, responsible SEO must not wait to react to new trends, but always keep integrating them into its Web search strategies.

Additionally, it is not only about incorporating better campaign formulas or marketing multimedia contents, local positioning thru geo-tagged keywords, social media strategies, and proper usages of SEO tools, etc., but also, conducting productive studies about the competition; and of course, learning to earn more SEO techniques that are significant to Google's ranking factors.

Based upon the ideas offered by the book's entirety, you will certainly feel confident forming your own SEO methodologies and strategies at the end— either for your personal applications or using them for your clients— upon answering to the following questions:

🖥 *What could or should be the most probable previews for SEO 2018?*

🖥 *What shall be the principal strategies you might be focusing upon?*

🖥 *How shall you build and develop your personal marketing strategies vis-à-vis the constant evolution of Google search and its latest innovations?*

🖥 *What could be certain features or aspects that could probably disrupt, or influence considerably in the era of SEO 2018?*

The contents presented herein constitute the rights of the First Amendment.

Presentation of the information is without binding contracts or any form of guarantees or assurances. It solely and strictly offers for informational purposes only; and as such, universal.

All information states to be truthful and consistent; in that, any liability, by way of inattention or otherwise, to any use or abuse of any policies, processes, or directions contained within, is the sole responsibility of the recipient reader.

If advice is necessary, consult a qualified professional for further questions concerning specific or critical matters on the subject.

Both author and publisher shall be, in no case, held liable for any fraud or fraudulent misrepresentations, monetary losses, damages, and liabilities— indirect, consequential, or special— arising from event/s beyond reasonable control, or relatively set out in this book.

Table of Contents

Top Ten Most Important Google Ranking Factors

CONCLUSION

CHAPTER 1 – INTRODUCTION TO SEO

"SEO is a relatively new, constantly evolving concept for Internet marketers. No marketing expert automatically knows how to play ball with SEO."
— **Matthew Cutts**, former head of Google's web spam team and current engineering director of the U.S. Digital Service

We believe that we could be bearing certain difficulties of achieving a comprehensive grasp about, or carrying a firm stance towards our confrontations and engagements with the recent and upcoming trends of SEO 2017 | 2018 lest we focus on revisiting or reviewing meticulously the fundamentals and technical understandings of search engine optimization (SEO), as well as how SEO really works.

Of course, every detail discussed hereafter will exclusively be within the boundaries and rigid confines of the just and fair white hat SEO practices— strictly adhering to all the primary search engine ideals, behaviors, rules, and policies.

SEO: A REDEFINITION

Foremost, we ought to begin redefining our basic understandings of SEO. It is truly a redefinition after SEO has already freed itself from its long-standing graying colors connoting the mysticisms and trickeries for both of its black and white hat practices in the Web. As Internet marketing professor, Chad Pollitt used to say, *"SEO is not something you do anymore. It is what happens when doing everything else right."*

Fact is that SEO has now become widely reputed as an essentially indispensable component of any upright digital marketing strategy or company. Its new definition is just actually tracing back to be living by, and up to its original functions and purposes.

SEO is quite simply the comprehensive term encompassing all the tactics and techniques, strategies and methodologies, and disciplinary practices that you may adopt and apply to assure your website's visibility, along with its contents and other significant details, on the search engine results pages (SERPs).

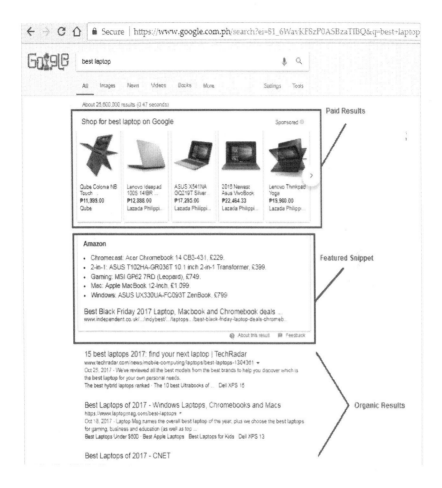

Image-1: SERP Common Details

Therefore, SEO is helping you out to position properly and advantageously your website to become immediately visible and easily searched out during the most crucial phases of the buying process; at oftentimes, prospective buyers pay your site a visit when they may need anything

SEO 2018

further through your site, or even when ordinary surfers merely want to feed their curiosities.

Speaking of visibility, it actually indicates how high up your website considerably ranks or appears in the SERP upon using certain keywords or search terms to produce the 'organic' results. Organic results denote those appearing naturally on the search page instead of emerging in the paid-for sections, as shown on Image-1

Paid-for results and featured snippets are also both essential in <u>search engine marketing</u>. Refer to the <u>guides for pay-per-click (PPC) and paid search</u>, and using featured snippets for further details.

SEO really sounds a lot simpler, especially when breaking down its strategies and processes used, which thereby, enables you to be more confident enough using the SEO term precisely.

However, SEO can be very technical, and oftentimes, following to a tee to whatever the primary search engines demand. Yet, like with most things, it only necessitates you to exert extra efforts working towards assuring the <u>optimization of your content</u> for consumption. Else, why even take time building your content when no one else would be searching for it?

The SEO strategies and processes used to boost visibility vary to certain extents— from the common (or traditional techniques) to the innovative technical practices (or new adaptations arising from the latest changes in search engine operations), which you may all accomplish on your website.

Additionally, all these applied works in the site also vary a lot— from their backside or behind-the-scene works (often referred to as, 'on-page SEO') to all their promotional work approaches such as social media marketing, link building, etc.(often referred to as, 'off-page SEO'.

PURPOSES AND SIGNIFICANCE OF SEO

Yet, more than being confident of using SEO properly and precisely is the realization of how important SEO is— the notably substantial percentage of how the search engines drive constant traffic to your website is a clear-cut indicator for the significance of SEO.

As a supplement for the figures in Image-2, recent studies further noted that 75% of all SEO traffic stemmed from organic searches, with only 6% produced from paid-for searches, while 2% arose from social media searches, and 12% and 15% came from direct and various referral sources respectively.

It is noteworthy that Google had cornered a little more than 90% of all the organic search traffic globally in 2015. Apparently, just by this overwhelming figure alone, your website should truly necessitate a very strong presence and visibility on Google SERPs.

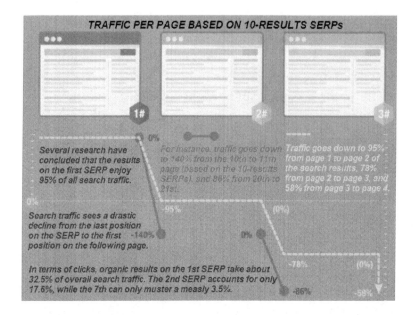

Image-2: Traffic per Page Based Upon 10-Results SERPs

For this reason, too, it goes to show how important indeed you need SEO to increase traffic to your site, or simply receive the highest chances possible for a broader readership base. As you know, it has always been paramount in digital marketing that heightened site traffic directly equates to higher sales and revenues.

Now, the question hangs upon how strong should then be your site's presence. Results obtained by Advanced Web Ranking (AWR)— a website rank-checking software— showed that the first five results on the primary SERP tally for about 67% of the total clicks while results on the 6th to 10th domains account for close to negligible clicks of 3.73%.

On the most fundamental of levels, your website is akin to a cake. The tempting icing would be your paid search, links, and social media network, but the major ingredients comprising the entire cake are the content, site infrastructure, information architecture, and content management system (CMS).

Every detail would seem indispensable that eliminating a single part would render your entire cake bland, dull, and considered fit for garbage disposal. As noted aptly by a funny meme circulating around the Web, *"The best place to hide a dead body is page 2 of Google search results!"*

Along with its significance, the ultimate goal of fundamental SEO is never to trick, tweak, or cheat all the search engines for your site's readability, ranking, and revisits, but:

⌨ To build an excellent, perfectly smooth, consistent, and coherent user experience (UX).

⌨ To convey to all the search engines all your pure intentions through the application of ideal SEO practices in order for them to recommend highly your website for direct and relevant searches.

Since SEO consists of several differing functions, as well as countless SEO services you may offer or avail, it is worthy to note the following trio of primary considerations, which are all about incorporating initially all your online marketing efforts, plans, and principal goals, prior to engaging with the ideal practices of the SEO proper.

DEFINE YOUR PLANNED BUSINESS FRAMEWORK

Concentrate and understand what would be your main objectives. You may need asking yourself the following questions to know better about your planned business model:

💻 Are you aware of both your assets and liabilities?

💻 What are your main objectives? (These goals refer to your personal aims, as well as to your website.)

💻 Are you in the business of persuading people to make 'impressions or eyeballs' (both terms interchangeably refer to the number of people visiting your website)

💻 Alternatively, are you engaged in a particular venture, which most people wanted to click?

💻 What exactly determines a 'conversion' (refers to any action occurring on your website that is more than valuable compared to anyone who just visits your site, then simply leaves sans doing anything) for you? Essentially, what comprises or represents a conversion depends entirely upon your entire plan.

OPTIMIZE PLANS FOR MULTI-CHANNEL NETWORKING

Application of basic SEO strategies such as keyword implementation is not only essential on-site, but also, it would be ideal to extend such strategies across various off-site channels like the following platforms:

- 🖥 Facebook;
- 🖥 Twitter;
- 🖥 Email or Google+;
- 🖥 LinkedIn or even Quora; and,
- 🖥 Offline channels, like TV, radio, and print ads.

Applying a consistency with your keyword phrases within these multi-channel networks not only augments your branding drives and campaigns but also familiarizes and instructs users to utilize specific keyword phrases you are optimizing for.

OPTIMIZE PLANS FOR MULTIMEDIA SOLUTIONS

Note well, Google created two indices for its search queries— one for desktop and the other for mobile devices. Thus, to attain a much wider reach, you need not only confine your optimization processes within the desktop experience, but also ensure <u>focusing optimization strategies on the latest search frontier enterprises— mobiles, tablets, and other innovative media.</u>

A common optimization strategy for multimedia usage is creating videos, audios, or other rich media non-text contents since it would be much easier landing all these rich Internet applications on the first SERP as opposed to plaintexts.

However, always ensure using the latest <u>readability practices of search engines,</u> to enable them crawling upon your contents— especially when using portable document formats (PDFs) or Adobe Flash applications.

Without having all these concrete website plans, your site will most likely fumble across the undesirable twin SEO page errors:

💻 301-page redirect, taking your users automatically to another page by clicking or entering your URL

💻 404-page error, arising from website malfunctions

"Marketing is not just billboards and TV ads anymore. Nowadays, the Internet is the primary source for gathering information, so search engine optimization has to be part of your marketing strategy in order for you to stay relevant online."

— Anonymous

Chapter 2 – SEO 101: Basic Guides To How White Hat SEO Works

"SEO gets the visitor to the door. It's up to your site's content to welcome and retain that visitor."
— **John I. Jerkovic**, IT Lead Consultant of the wealth management company, Sengual

Search engine optimization consultant, Jill Whalen once remarked, *"Only search engine tricks need to keep changing when the ranking algorithms change."* Thus, echoing Matt Cutts' same observation expressed at first chapter's opening quote, one could never be an expert in SEO since its practices evolve constantly with respect to the equally evolving changes and innovations of search engines.

What is always sure and constant is that everyone can actually perform all the various SEO practices... and perform them right and proper.

SEO does not really connote an activity of rocket science that it takes you arduous years of studying it. You only need to know the basics and soar eventually from there. Jill Whalen continues to say, *"Good SEO work only gets better over time."*

Laying out the basic guidelines of SEO provides you what you truly need to soar higher; at the same time, it enables you to understand better, how an ideal SEO works— fulfilling objectives of boosting your website traffic— to either increase sales of your products or simply, reach a wider base of readership.

Foremost, you have to understand about the traffic trap so that, in turn, you may know the actual dealings of SEO. Many digital marketers often misconstrue viewing SEO specifically as the root for creating free traffic. While it is all true that free traffic is the result of SEO, it is not how SEO typically functions.

The true intention of SEO is helping users searching for you, or your site, in particular, to find it easily. Achieving such purpose would be matching your website's contents to what users are trying to search. Bear in mind what the successful SEO practitioner, Aaron Wall revealed, *"The success of a page should be measured by a single criterion: does the visitor do what you want them to do?"* For instance:

John sells custom-made scented candles. You can see on his blog how he makes the candles manually, at oftentimes, relating to the various fragrances he uses.

The keyword competition in terms of fragrances slacks and John keeps publishing several great contents about them. Sooner than he realized, his site landed high rankings on the first SERPs for many various kinds of fragrances.

The potential cause for concern here is that users looking for the same fragrances, which John uses, are most likely making scented candles themselves. Worse, it would be much unlikely for them becoming inclined to purchase John's candles. Yes, he receives a huge volume of traffic, yet, nothing ever converts because visitors or users have entirely different goals.

Thus, your first lesson learned here is ensuring your goals match properly those of your users if you desire SEO working effectively for you. It is never about the traffic, but conversion.

It means determining what you truly want, then optimizing the want with keywords, which lure users wanting the same. However, aside from keywords, effective SEO entails a lot more details.

1 – FINDING THE PROPER AND PERTINENT KEYWORDS

Researching for the proper and pertinent keywords is the primordial step towards a highly successful SEO strategy. Fact is that, almost everything in your site orbits around your keywords.

The world of SEO defines a keyword as, *"an abstraction or conceptual word, extrapolated from multiple search queries."* Thus, it is a certain word, which users use for searching specific subjects on search engines.

Hence, when you are marketing a particular product, all your keywords used should have an affinity or association to your product and, as much as possible, identified by universally, when wanting your products appearing in user's searches. The keywords you use are what drive your target traffic to your products.

Several online tools are available to help you search the right keywords. Foremost among these keyword researcher tools is the widely renowned Google Search-Based Keyword Tool.

Begin brainstorming and researching your possible keywords, and compare for yourself how they fare with the competition through using the Keyword Planner tool from Google AdWords.

Apparently, performing your keyword research could somehow be mind-numbing; yet, it is vitally necessary for your proper keyword searching process.

To facilitate you further, work and bring out keywords with the following ideal attributes:

🖥 Possess a steep search volume; meaning, users identify and search your chosen keywords

🖥 Possess relevance to your site or have the support of your site's content

🖥 Possess low competency levels; meaning, they have fewer results, which in turn means, having greater chances of ranking higher

Nonetheless, upon noticing that some of your chosen keywords are highly competitive within your site's niche, it is highly advisable to apply for long-tail keywords, which makes it easier for your site to rank higher in the SERPs.

LONG TAIL KEYWORD

The long tail keyword describes a remarkable keyword creation process, whereby, a combination of several low-traffic keywords delivers potentially more visitors instead of using fewer high-traffic keywords.

Typically, long tail keywords are phrases, consisting usually of two to five or even more keywords. The longer they are, the better, since you will have lesser competition for such particular phrases against the generic keywords in the search engines.

Besides, these types of keywords are very straightforward and specific to whatever products you sell. Whenever a user uses a very specific keyword search phrase, chances are that they are searching precisely for what they are virtually planning to buy.

The bottom line is that targeting long tail key phrases will definitely lead to results that are more profitable. Apparently, the profitability stems from these following important reasons:

🖥 Facilitates your site towards higher rankings

🖥 Lead to higher sales conversions of visitors

🖥 Enables more pages for indexing in Google

However, it would be very disadvantageous for you if you keep focusing and dabbling too much in creating long tail key phrases that are too specific, if not, too common. As it is the case, you are bringing your key phrases to a highly competitive search, which reduces your chances of meriting higher rankings.

Thus, it is even highly possible that you will never receive sufficient traffic for sustaining your business. For this reason, it would really be ideal to have either:

🖥 Fewer indexed pages providing you a huge volume of lowly targeted traffic; or,

🖥 Greater number of indexed pages, each providing you a lesser volume of highly targeted traffic

You may instead view the idealism through this perspective: Do you rather intend to rank your site for using only a single keyword that accounted to deliver a thousand visitors daily, OR, targeting about a hundred long tail keywords, half of which delivering you a single buyer daily?

2 – Creating Quality Content

It has long been a buzzword in SEO circles that content is king. Foremost, quality content brings to the table the following significant reasons to support its royal stature in SEO practice:

🖥 Cultivates the Ideals of SEO Purposes – High quality and unique content for your product's website or blog influences SEO greatly, as well as the rankings in the search engine for two main reasons:

On one hand, publishing regularly 300- to 500-word count quality contents, with naturally placed or stuffed keywords and built-in internal links that lead to other pertinent contents, facilitates your website ranking organically for relevant keywords and search terms.

 Ultimately, a higher ranking practically exposes your brand to more users and prospects looking for good contents in your niche.

On the other hand, it builds your authority in the niche, and thus, opening windows for creating an enthusiastic backlink profile.

🖥 Promotes User Engagement – High quality and unique content, regardless of form—text or non-text— encourages user engagements with your brand, either consciously or not.

Users eagerly take time out empathizing with your brand message, digesting your entire content, and perhaps, even sharing, liking, or commenting your content. Otherwise, poor contents only prompt users to keep scrolling past until your content becomes lost into oblivion.

🖥 Generates Fresh Leads and Conversions – High quality and unique contents build brand authority and exposure in a very saturated market. With more consumers becoming aware of your brand, your site certainly gains strong potentials of generating new leads and increasing sales conversions.

Generally, good contents characterize less of the blatant and straightforward marketing pitches, yet, remain seemingly advertorial with its theme. This urges consumers to engage sincerely with your brand sans any conspicuous sales messages, which often disrupt their engagements.

Furthermore, contents, written and presented in an editorial or journalistic reporting style, foster the growth of the consumers' relationship with your brand, evolving from their present status as ordinary consumers to valued clients to brand advocates.
On the contrary, product-oriented contents only annoy consumers and produce negative effects on their relationship and impressions with your brand.

🖥 Contributes More Value to Your Product – High quality and unique content— particularly in the form of an informative post about your product, a how-to blog entry, a webinar or an instructional video— adds a great sense of value to your product or service. Consumers generally welcome such content for reasons that it influences greatly their lives, imparts with them new information, and somehow, resolves a problem in their daily living.

Obviously, the value gained is intangible. It does not entail any direct monetary worth, but of course, it is invaluable to your business framework, as well as to the budding relationship between the consumers and your brand.

🖥 Enhances Website Traffic and User Experience – High quality and unique content are also excellent means of driving traffic to your website while retaining them for longer durations on the site or prompting them for further revisits.

For instance, a website appearing with only a home and contact page virtually receives very limited page views, high bounce rates (visiting, then leaving immediately), and few user engagements. Contrariwise, a website appearing with an onsite blog filled with entertaining and engaging contents projects positive impressions upon the users while encouraging them to visit multiple pages and interact with the site's interface.

For all these reasons, the common denominator that bestows upon the content its kingly crown is focusing on its high quality, unique, and authentic creations that entertain, spark interests and contribute value for consumers. For turning out such content creations, put emphases on:

🖥 Titles and Subtitles / Taglines – Eye-catching or intriguing titles stimulate reader's interest. Capitalize on a great initial impression at the first instance.

🖥 Originality and Structure – Uniqueness and quality of content prompt users visiting your site since they cannot find easily a similar content elsewhere. Structure refers to ease of readability with inclusions of headings, subheadings, and lists.

🖥 Freshness and Timelessness – Although it is great publishing content that remains relevant to the changing times, you should also keep adding new content regularly. You can consider introducing a blog or Q & A section of your website if time does not permit you to create high quality and unique contents.

⌨ Keyword Selection – Choose the right and relevant keywords in your content to bring users to your site.

⌨ Link Building – Build links to quality sites, which complement contents of your page. This encourages other sites within your niche linking to yours as well.

⌨ Unique and Plagiarized-Free – Never publish copied, plagiarized, or duplicate contents, else, search engines imposes your site with penalties.

3 – OPTIMIZING WEBSITE CODES

Not only do search engine bots read the texts of your website, but they also read evaluating your website codes written in hypertext markup language (HTML). For this reason, you need to optimize the following eight different areas of your codes:

CODING META TITLE TAGS

Title tags enclose the official title of your website. Helping you demonstrate optimization points for your title tags, consider the following code examples used from two popular global web design services outfits— webdesignerdepot.com and iconcept.com.ph— which both take differing approaches in their respective site code markups. First, look at webdesignerdepot.com:

Image-3: Meta Title Tag Code for webdesignerdepot.com

As you will notice, the author stressed the site's name and niche. When you look for it in search engines, you may possibly enter searching directly for, "Web Design" or "Webdesigner Depot."

Looking at the counterpart's iconcept.com.ph site:

Image-4: Meta Title Tag Code for iconcept.com.ph

The author of iconcept.com took a more different approach. As the author included its location to its niche, it emphasized the major essentials of what the website distinctively implies. Most likely, you would find it by searching specifically for, "Web Design in the Philippines," or any proximate variation thereof.

Therefore, when you code your title tags, it all boils down to ensuring the title includes your primary keywords. Optimizing further the search engine results, each page of your website must bear a distinctively unique title tag, which should not exceed 70 characters in length.

SPECIFYING META DESCRIPTION TAGS

The meta-description tag is to provide a curt summary that describes specifically the content of your webpage.

Essentially, it bears no impact on the rankings in the SERPs, but its importance lies upon letting users know what your site is all about by reading the brief description appearing just below your meta-title tag in the SERP. Refer to Images 5 & 6 below for the same site examples.

Webdesigner Depot: Web Design Blog
https://www.webdesignerdepot.com/ ▼
Web Design Resources for Web Designers. We include Photoshop Tutorials, WordPress Plugins, and Web Development tools. Download free icons, Photoshop ...

Image-5: Meta Description Tag Code for webdesignerdepot.com

Web Design Philippines | Trusted Digital Marketing Company
iconcept.com.ph/ ▼
One-stop web design and digital marketing company in Manila, Philippines offering web design, mobile app, SEO, SMM, PPC and other digital solutions.
SEO Philippines · Graphic Design and Motion ... · Contact Us · About Us

Image-6: Meta Description Tag Code for iconcept.com

Hence, with a unique description and proper formatting, your meta-description tags strategize to increase your click-through rates (CTRs), or the percentage of users who really click on your website.

Although search engines have currently ignored the use of meta-keywords, they are still important because your keywords guide you to create your meta-description tags. Besides, keywords used indicate the specificities and nature of your website. Observe the emphases of the meta-keywords of the same site examples in their respective meta- description tags:

For webdesignerdepot.com:

35

```
<meta-name="keywords" content="web design, web
designer, Photoshop, graphic design, CSS, illustrator,
twitter, photography, free icons, WordPress, web
developer, web development" />
```

```
<meta-name="description" content=" "Web Design
Resources for Web Designers. We include Photoshop
Tutorials, WordPress Plugins, and Web Development tools.
Download free icons, Photoshop brushes." />
```

The site was very comprehensive by citing more of their
services other than their flagship expertise, web design.
Searching for "web design" in Google,
webdesignerdepot.com shows up right on the first SERP.
Other sites with equally variegated web design services
also prop up like behance.com and courser.com. Thus,
when having several online service interests, you might
wish to take such keyword and meta-description
approach.

For iconcept.com.ph:
```
<meta-name="keywords" content=" one-stop web design,
digital marketing company, web designer in the
Philippines, mobile app, SEO, SMM, PPC, digital solutions"
/>
```

```
<meta-name="description" content="One-stop web design
and digital marketing company in Manila, Philippines
offering web design, mobile app, SEO, SMM, PPC and
other digital solutions." />
```

The site practically made a complete sentence out of their
keywords. It emphasized clearly the type of user it wanted

visiting their site by specifying the location of their offered services. Hence, upon searching for "web designer in the Philippines" in Google, iconcept.com.ph ranks topmost in the first SERP. This approach would suitably suit you, especially if you want your services to cater exclusively to people in a certain location.

Therefore, when creating your meta-tag descriptions in complete sentences, ensure that your keywords situate well in the description. It is ideal keeping your meta-descriptions longer in order to be sufficiently defining and descriptive, but never exceed its 160-character limit; else, the search engine compels cutting it off.

Moreover, try making, as much as possible, a unique meta-description for each page of your site. In this manner, you will be gaining higher possibilities of users discovering more about your site.

STRUCTURING THE HEADINGS

Akin to headings found in articles or books (either larger, bolder or underlined fonts), site headings are anchors guiding readers through the text. Without them, texts are terrible to read. Thus, its principal purpose is making the text more readable.

Headings follow a specific and chronological order: h1, h2, h3, h4, h5 and so on. The first heading code, h1, starts as the principal heading on your page. The subsequent heading codes go down to sub-level headings on your site. For instance:

```
<h1>SEO 101: Basic Guides to How White Hat SEO Works</h1>
    <h2>Finding the Proper and Pertinent Keywords</h2>
        <h3>Long Tail Keyword<h3>
    <h2>Creating Quality Content</h2>
    <h2>Optimizing Website Codes</h2>
            <h3>Coding Meta Title Tags</h3>
            <h3>Specifying Meta Description Tags</h3>
            <h3>Structuring the Headings</h3>
            <h3>Creating and Submitting Sitemaps</h3>
            <h3>Choosing the Domain Name and Extension </h3>
            <h3>Factoring the URL Structure</h3>
            <h3>Adding of Alt Tags</h3>
    <h2>Building White Label and Cross Links</h2>
    <h2>Essential White Hat SEO Techniques</h2>
            <h3>On-Page Optimization</h3>
            <h3>Off-Page Optimization</h3>
```

Image-7: Hierarchal Structure of Headings and Sub-Level Headings

Apparently, the perceptual structure denotes, the more specific and detailed your content is, the higher will be the corresponding heading's number.

Generally, each page should only have a single h1 or main heading tag, and then, you can make as many sub-level headings of h2s, h3s, etc., as necessary. More importantly, ensure that your headings include keywords, which are relevant to your site's content.

Despite the fact that both headings and subheadings are not prime ranking factors, they influence greatly SEO because of their importance of facilitating users to understand your text. Besides, they help readers for easy access to certain topics of your content. In short, headings are very useful for organizing and structuring your entire texts.

Therefore, if readers use them as they so intend, so does Google. By that means, headings heighten the possibilities of users to read actually your article, as well as improve accessibility to your contents.

CREATING AND SUBMITTING SITEMAPS

Sitemaps are special documentary codes you create yourself, or from certain free software, which provide search engine bots a sort of a roadmap of the structure and organization of all your website pages.

The sitemap facilitates these bots efficiently in finding everything on your site; and thereby, finally indexing them to display your pages on the Internet. You can create sitemaps in two different types:

⌨ HTML Sitemaps – form sets of specific markup codes and symbols that describe file and page contents (chiefly, text and graphic images) to make it easier for users to read.

If your site has a few hundred pages, you must link every page in your HTML sitemap to give your visitors an overview of about everywhere they wish to go. Yet, if your site contains a few thousand or more pages, you may only have to link those essential pages.

⌨ XML (Extensible Markup Language) Sitemaps – form the same sets of specific markup codes and symbols as HTML sitemaps, only that, they are self-defining or the data itself embeds the data structure, making it easier for both users and machines to read. Even if your site comprises a million pages, you can link every page of your site in your XML sitemap.

Several free XML sitemap generator tools found online can help you create your sitemap. Among the top three most recommended are the following:

❖ www.xml-sitemaps.com

❖ xmlsitemapgenerator.org

❖ www.web-site-map.com

You will then submit your creation to Google Webmaster Central Portal to allow all the search engines crawling and indexing your site.

Nevertheless, many misinterpret an XML sitemap is responsible for having site pages indexed. Google does not pursue indexation processes of your pages just because you requested them. Actually, Google only inclines to index your pages because:

🖥 It found your pages (meaning, your pages have the proper formatting and structure), and consequently, crawled onto them.

🖥 It considered and regarded your pages to have good quality, which is worthy of indexing.

Therefore, your submission of the XML sitemap to the Google Search Console only means that you are giving Google a clue about the propriety and quality that your pages bear.

CHOOSING THE DOMAIN NAME AND EXTENSION

Among the primary and most crucial decisions to make when starting or creating a new website is choosing your domain name. Your choice influences the success of your site in almost every aspect, including SEO and social media marketing (SMM).

A domain name containing your focus keywords ranks higher as opposed to those without keywords. What even ranks higher is an exact match domain (EMD).

EMDs exactly match verbatim the keyword or phrase targeted to users. However, EMDs entail certain costs since you usually have to purchase them (usually at godaddy.com or namecheap.com). Additionally, EMDs do not generally bear uniqueness.

For this reason, several companies create and use new and invented words or phrases as their domain name so they can build a brand around it, rather than belaboring to explain the existing definition.

Whichever may be ideal and better actually depends on your SEO marketing plans and strategies:

⌨ If the bulk of your user traffic comes plainly from search engines, then using a quality EMD may be a wise decision. For example, if you are wanting to rank for 'travel,' then 'travel.com' will surely rank well at the top of SERPs due to its keyword-rich domain name.

⌨ If your marketing formulation includes only a small part of SEO, then you may rather devise a more creative and unique domain name. 'Google' seemed an alien word then, but it has become a big household brand now.

Many free domain name generators found online can help you come up discovering your domain or business name. Among the top three most recommended are the following:

❖ www.leandomainsearch.com

❖ www.namemesh.com

❖ www.wordoid.com

If you want to create your domain name by yourself, the following are helpful tips to guide you:

⌨ Keep your domain name short, simple, and memorable, or, bearing an easy recall. One or a couple of words is ideal. On average, the domain names of the top 100,000 sites only carry nine characters. In addition, keep it easy to spell and pronounce.

⌨ Be aware of e-commerce trademarks to avoid trouble. Ensure your domain name is not, or never comes close to a domain or trademark of others. Changing your domain name unexpectedly must be the last thing you want to happen after founding and building your brand online.

⌨ Devise a more creative, unique, original, and marketable brand for your domain name. This can never be an easy task, but it all starts with dissecting the root or nature of your product, service, or brand. You may begin trying the following:

❖ Compound whole words (Facebook), or make a portmanteau (Pin + Interest = Pinterest),

❖ Tweak or misspell a word (Reddit = Read It),

❖ Use a phrase (The Free Dictionary),

❖ Affix a word with either a prefix or a suffix (Spotify),

❖ Make up a unique word (Ojoo).

Soon after registering your domain name, you may want to consider registering it further with either a single or several country-specific domain extensions just like, iconcept.com.ph.

A country-specific extension in your domain name can enhance the marketing and branding perspectives of your site, making visitors from a targeted country more comfortable with your site or brand right from the start. It actually helps your site rank better.

FACTORING THE URL STRUCTURE

Many SEO practitioners fail to notice the importance of the universal resource locator (URL). Maybe because, they oftentimes interchange domain names and URLs, perceiving both terms mean the same.

For all you know, the domain name is the web address of your site. Essentially, it consists of the site's name separated by a dot with the top-level domain name, usually, com (for commerce), which is the gold standard for top-level domain names (i.e., yoursitename.com).

On the other hand, the URL is actually the web address of a particular page on your website. Meaning, your website will have as many URLs as its pages. Structurally, it consists chronologically of the computer language or protocol (hypertext transfer protocol or HTTP), domain name, and path, also known as, port.

Generally, you mark the port invisible, since the default port for the HTTP protocol always remains as 80 (i.e., http://yoursitename.com).

When you have disorderly or inappropriate URLs, search engines incur difficulties to crawl them; and thus, disabling them to index your web pages, and consequentially, losing your chance to rank in the SERPs.

Ensuring your URLs to be more search-friendly, factor them out using the following parameters:

⌨ Only use letters and numbers, and never use impertinent and immaterial characters in structuring your URLs (! @ # $ % ? * = _). Search engines rather opt for reading dashes.

⌨ Typically, shorter URLs rank higher compared to longer ones. You can avail free URL shortening services online such as bitly.com, goo.gl.com, and tinyurl.com

SEO 2018

🖥 Sub-domains structured in the URL can rank higher as opposed to using sub-directories.

As a primer, on one hand, any extension separated by a slash of your main domain name is a sub-directory, also called as a sub-folder (i.e., http://www.yourSLD.com/about-us/ where, 'about us' is a sub-directory of your domain name.

On the other hand, a sub-domain is another level added before the domain name, also known technically as, second-level domain (SLD), in the URL.

By default, every top-level domain name has 'www (World Wide Web)' as sub-domain. However, you can generally replace the default sub-domain, www, only for the following reasons:

🖥 If you want to build your site catering to different languages, then you specify the particular language your site serves (i.e., http://jp.yourSLD.com where, 'jp' refers to the Japanese language).

🖥 When franchising your site, you want to help your franchisees by providing them their own respective sites, and let them stay in the same SLD as you are in (i.e., http://locationoffranchisee.yourSLD.com).

🖥 If you have a wide array of products, then you can indicate a particular product as your sub-domain (i.e., http://producttype.yourSLD.com).

Therefore, a sub-domain would be ideal if you do not want your site pages indexed altogether with your SLD pages. Placing those excluded pages in a subfolder denotes that its indexation comes from the same site.

ADDING ALT TAGS

Optimizing a website always hinges upon balancing between driving in larger volumes of traffic and improving continuously the user experience (UX). Truly, it is a delicate balance requiring the determination of the proper applications of text against graphics.

Since Google and other search engines can never read actual images, you can help them reading out by adding or inserting an alt tag or alt text (alternative text) in your site's HTML code document.

The alt tag appears in a tooltip or infotip— a tan-colored, boxed, text snippet, normally superimposed on the image (upon you hover your mouse over a certain image of a page). Refer to Image-8 for a descriptive detail of the alt tag interface element.

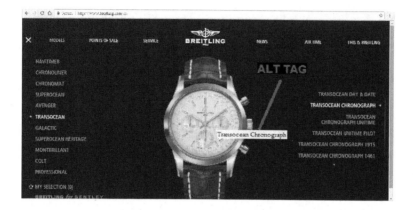

Image-8: Alt Tag Details

Actually, the text gives alternative information about the image to the viewers, especially, to visually impaired users, who avail the help of a screen reader to enable them accessing and reading the information.

The alt text also facilitates viewers, who are unable to see the image due to either a slow connection or certain errors in the source code file computing (src) attribute that disables displaying the image.

For every image in a page, the alt tag code describes to search engines the inclusive data and attributes of the image. For the alt tag code of the above example:

```
<img data-
src="https://cdn2.breitling.com/media/image/0/base/asse
t-version-4ef8261c1b/transocean-chronograph-3.png"
alt="Breitling Transocean Chronograph"/>
```

The src attribute denotes the image's URL. As a web page loads, the browser receives from a web server the details of the image and adds it to the page.

When performed properly, adding alt tags not only enhances your user's experiences but also, helps search engines recognizing one of your most significant contents— high definition and striking colored images— that compels users to read more or stay on your page. Otherwise, when done improperly, Google penalizes your site.

Herewith are your procedures for adding the alt text to your images:

Step-1: Click 'Edit' or double-click the Gallery Block of your site.

Step-2: Locate the image you wish to edit. Hover your mouse over it, and then, click the 'Add alt text to the Image Title box'.

Step-3: Type your relevant text on the box, describing the image, and then, click 'Save.'

4 – BUILDING WHITE LABEL AND CROSS LINKS

White label links are web pages created by secondary sources, after which, other websites or companies will brand these links as their own.

In essence, it is actually an outsourcing process, whereby, you hire another entity to perform for you other important side tasks and allied works for optimizing your site.

Many companies practice this process, mainly, to widen their base and reach online; at the same time, to make the most of their capital resources since the process takes lots of expertise, expenses, and time.

Aside from engaging with the economic and prudent practice of building white label links, it is also important for you to apply the art of cross-linking your website.

Cross-linking is a strategy of linking a certain page to another within your site. For details, it is placing anchor texts or the clickable hyperlink on certain texts of the content on your webpage that leads users to connect to another page on your website.

Links are perhaps, the most important aspect of your SEO practice. The high value of links in SEO allows for you easy researching and creation or modification of your contents while improving your users' experiences for giving them the comforts and conveniences of grasping better your site's intents.

Furthermore, your web pages will certainly rank higher when several websites link to your own website.

Although it would be close to impossible to persuade thousands, much less, hundreds of websites linking to your own site, you just really have to keep producing quality contents to entice visitors or make an impact on the Web with your contents.

From the perspectives of search engines, they see and regard you and your site as having more authority on your contents when more trustworthy and relevant sites link to you.

Prior to building your links, the following are general pointers you should always remember when optimizing your site using links:

🖥 The more effective links are links placed within your contents rather than links found in your site's footer or sidebar.

🖥 Keep the number of your links or anchor texts for each web page below 100, lest incurring sanctions from Google.

🖥 Google appreciates your site more when linking from other related sites instead of from unreliable or irrelevant sites, which have no quality contents (i.e., outgoing or external links to a Feedburner page or a web content management tools page).

🖥 Irrelevant also include links to your terms of service and other no-bearing pages. Hence, if you want to block such pages, you just exclude them in your robots.txt file (the text file you create to instruct search engine bots how to crawl pages on your site).

🖥 Reciprocal links (you link to others and the same link to you) render to be ineffective. Google discourages such practice because it doubts about a mutual solicitation of links.

🖥 Aside from soliciting for links, purchasing text links can get your site banned from search engines.

ESSENTIAL WHITE HAT SEO TECHNIQUES

SEO covers a wide range of technical practices, with which search engines regard some as dishonest or unfair while considering others as honest, fair, and precisely proper in representing contents of a site.

On one hand, the unfair SEO practices of digital marketing, termed as black hat techniques, render sometimes a short-lived boost to page views and rankings; but oftentimes, at the expense of low-quality traffic and search engine sanctions.

On the other hand, the fair SEO practices of digital marketing, termed as white hat techniques, are among the ideal ways of promoting a brand and business, as well as managing site traffic, because of their long-term success and sustainability.

The gray areas surrounding these contrasting SEO practices, aptly called as gray hat techniques are the practices of SEO techniques and strategies, which remain undefined or accredited by published parameters from Google, and for which many logical SEO practitioners might yet disagree on the means and manners by which these techniques contrast or support the published authoritative guidelines of Google.

Generally, all these SEO practices funnel down to two major components: on-page and off-page SEO techniques.

ON-PAGE OPTIMIZATION

On-page optimization denotes the scope of measures and standards, with which you undertake internally or directly within your blog or website to boost its rankings from its current position in the SERP.

Thus, it is undergoing the processes of updating and optimizing your essential page elements like the following:

❖ Content (Fresh and High Quality)
❖ External Links (No Links to 'Spam-my' Sites)
❖ Image Optimization (Use of Alt Tag)
❖ Internal Links (Cross-Linking)
❖ Text Formatting (Use of Headings)
❖ Titles and Descriptions (Keyword-Rich)
❖ URL Structures (Proper Coding)
❖ User-Friendly Navigation (User Sitemaps)
❖ User-Friendly 404 Pages
❖ Fast-Loading Pages
❖ Mobile-Friendly Pages

OFF-PAGE OPTIMIZATION

Off-page optimization denotes the scope of measures and standards, with which you undertake externally from your blog or website to boost its rankings from its current position in the SERP.

Thus, it is undergoing the processes of acquiring as many high-quality backlinks or incoming links as you can, like the following:

❖ Link Building / Link Baiting
❖ Social Bookmarking
❖ Social Media Marketing

🖥 Link Building – is not only among the most important factors in SEO but also, among the most abused aspect of improving site rankings.

Through the years since the advent of SEO, webmasters have always been putting too much emphasis on building links to their sites in the hopes of achieving top rankings, and thereby, concocted several ways for increasing link count.

Among the most notorious were:

❖ Blog Directories – similar to the Yellow Pages telephone directory, but each entry carried a link, which pointed back to a website.

❖ Forum Signatures – included certain links of users when they commented in online forums. The purpose of which was to get a link back to their site.

❖ Comment Link – shared a similar concept with forum signatures where users included their links in their comments on a certain blog or website to get a link back to their site.

What has been worse and too abusive was using keywords in lieu of their real names (i.e., they wrote 'How to Start Your Own Business' instead of their real identity, John Doe).

❖ Article Directories – assured users who published their articles to these directories for receiving a link or two back to their websites. Only a few article directories accepted exclusively unique, original, and standard quality contents.

However, many directories accommodated anything, from spinning to previously published articles, to even nonsensical, low quality, and improperly structured manuscripts.

❖ Shared Content Directories – such as InfoBarrel and HubPages allowed users to publish their contents, as well as adding a couple of links pointing back to the users' websites.

⚑ WARNING ⚑
All these link-building methods described no longer work nowadays. You must not even take a shot doing any of them; else, Google bans you.

Since link building became a very easy means towards manipulating the algorithms of search engines, Google has only become much smarter and smarter in detecting all these black hat techniques.

Through Google's recent introductions of the Hummingbird, Penguin, and Panda algorithms, it has now managed to resolve a huge part of these issues while protecting their SERPs from spammers and irresponsible users.

Nonetheless, there will always be exceptions, like a clever rat finding its way to escape. For this reason, Google has been updating continuously and tirelessly each release of their novel algorithms to render all these black hat SEO techniques extinct.

While there may be more proper ways of optimizing your links, today's practices midst the perpetual innovations of search engines only compel you enhancing more of the traditional dynamic strategies— internal (cross-linking) and external link building.

To realize both of them successfully, it all leads you back to producing regularly a high quality and new content for your site that is worth linking. Meaning, your content must always be unique, original, and useful.

The ideal way for such an execution is through starting a blog. Thereby, you should explore more about link baiting— the process of creating quality and authoritative contents, which users want to share.

🖥 Link Baiting – becomes a sure bet for optimizing your links while ranking higher in the light of the constantly changing search engine algorithms. Here are your systematic procedures for a successful link baiting process:

❖ Start your contents or articles by knowing what your audience or viewers like or found it useful and interesting to share or recommend to others. Certain tools such as Ahrefs and Buzzsumo can help you search for these popular topics.

Of course, you also have to do a lot of research on these topics. These highly shared contents imply the existence of their strong demand, and thus, making it easier for you to get more links.

❖ After creating your highly shared topic, apply the Skyscraper Technique— a continuous process of improving more of the successful article— by performing either of the following:

1. Extend – Generally, these highly shared articles are in the form of roundup lists such as, 'Top Ten Movies' or '15 Most Nutritious Foods.' You can improve your roundup lists by extending the, perhaps, doubling the number of your entries.

2. Update – Published contents online remain living forever on the Web. Meaning, they will also age and incur high possibilities of being outdated. Thus, you need to update your published contents regularly with more relevant and fresher information, as well as links to ensure their sustained usefulness to your audience.

3. Add Sources or Details – Perhaps, you might have come across pieces of your contents listed with only a little to no references or details at all. Expound each point and add sources, even if each point only contains a statement or

two. This makes your content much more authoritative and valuable.

4. Makeover – Properly structured contents for easy reading plus an excellently designed page will most likely lure visitors to having a great experience reading, staying comfortably on your site, and sharing your contents. Hence, try undergoing a complete makeover of your content structures and inserting high-quality visuals and elements on your pages.

5. Promote – Engaging your content across all your social media accounts promotes linking and sharing with your social media audience.

6. Outreach – Your final step to undertake is disputably the most difficult stage of link building— outreach. Begin by researching the competition since this is your best guarantee of having users willing and interested to link back to your site.

Avail using the Open Site Explorer tool to search for sites that point to your competitors. Never mind referring pages such as directories and forums. Thus, by using the tool, you will now discover a list of sites that are:

❖ Linking to your site, or interested in your niche or business,
❖ Currently on-topic; and,
❖ Previously linking to contents similar to your own, but apparently inferior in quality and structure.

By having this significant information, you can then discover new possibilities and opportunities for obtaining new links for your own site.

In addition, the Open Site Explorer, through its Check My Links extension tool, allows you to discover also broken links invalid links that redirects to your URL, or any page in your site having 404-page errors so that you can promptly check and fix the problem.

Knowing your competition, especially identifying those sites that have the greatest authority, you can now aim at them to raise your chances of obtaining the most valuable links. You should also use the following tools while you generate your outreach list:

❖ BlogDash – helps you search for bloggers in your niche. More importantly, it provides you their contact information, as well as their most recent writings.

❖ AuthorCrawler – helps you search for links to a page, upon which the tool crawls them to scan for the author markup and show their Google+ information.

When disseminating outreach emails, streamline your procedures by devising a general template for writing to bloggers about persuading them with your article as a supplement to their erstwhile post.

Usually, you may only receive a few responses from the bloggers you have reached out. Persevere and never be discouraged. Bear in mind that you have contacted them due to their high authority and a large following. Meaning, a little bit can always go a long, long way in terms of the value passed by their respective links.

🖥 Social Media Marketing – Social media is not only a part of off-page SEO techniques but it is also a type of link building. Although most links you obtain from social media are no-follow links (links that do not boost your page rankings), they do not translate that they have nothing of value.

Fact is that social media citations are revving up to be ranking factors in the near future by simply implementing the proper configurations of social media profiles.

Engaging with other social media sites like the news aggregator, digg.com, or stumbleupon.com, which searches and recommends contents to users, do not just drive huge volumes of traffic to your site. Your site's increased visibility can raise your chances for other users to link to your site.

🖥 Social Bookmarking – Although social bookmarking is no longer as popular as before, it is still a reliable way to drive traffic to your site. Depending on your business industry type or niche, you may find trustworthy websites for promoting your content such as delicious.com, stumbleupon.com, scoop.it.com, reddit.com, etc.

In conclusion, both off-page and on-page optimization techniques are truly very significant in SEO. You just ought to perform both practices to succeed in your SEO campaigns.

In terms of link building, prudence dictates: never go the easy way or undergo shortcuts; but rather, try obtaining links from difficult places. The greater the difficulties in obtaining your links, the higher value they always have.

Before, one could easily obtain countless links and immediately rank higher. You can no longer do that nowadays.

For all you know, the best advice would be forgetting altogether all about link building, and rather gather and place all your efforts in creating a great website:

❖ Try figuring out what people like and are looking for

❖ Build your site devoted to their needs

❖ Optimize your site for search engines so that they will lead people finding you

❖ Promote your site in the most proper ways

❖ ...and everything else follows!

If you only implement all of the best practices and advice mentioned, you will definitely increase your traffic from search engines. Be patient as ever. After all, search engines take time updating their records, with billions of sites to crawl.

Also, bear in mind that it takes time figuring out what really works for you and your website. What became feasible and worked for others may not be the same as yours.

There are no shortcuts or speeding things up. Otherwise, the long arm of the search engines' laws is bound to catch you! It is never worth it.

Hard work and adhering to the ideal SEO principles always pay off. However, it is not all about smart SEO. It is all about what search engines always want you to do.

In the end, their objective is having all the excellent websites for every niche showing up on top. Therefore, if you only work hard to build the best website and promote it ideally and effectively, search engines will eventually catch up.

Nevertheless, everything you have read at this point is just the tip of the iceberg. Gaining a profound understanding of SEO vis-à-vis approaching the continuous innovations of search engines is answering these following questions:

What are search engines looking for, and not looking for? How can you build your website in such a way that it pleases your visitors, as well as your demanding friends— Google, Yahoo, Bing, and other search engines? Most importantly, how can SEO help your web presence become more profitable midst the seemingly perpetual changing algorithms?

"If you have an outstanding product, world-class content, or something else that sets you apart, then you can step back and start thinking about how to promote it. Google wants people doing white hat search engine optimization (or even no search engine optimization at all) to be free to focus on creating amazing, compelling websites."
— **Matthew Cutts**

CHAPTER 3 – FUNCTIONALITIES OF GOOGLE

"My rule of thumb is building a site for a user, not a spider."
— **Dave Naylor**, Founder of the full-service digital marketing agency, Bronco

As search engines evolve, so goes with SEO. Fact is that the life and soul of SEO are all dependent upon the dynamics and functionalities of search engines.

Why do search engines change? It is simply because; people and their behaviors also change. These changes prompt technology to evolve in order to keep up with the changing needs and wants of people.

That said, it would be important to have even a bird's eye view about the existence of search engines so that SEO would know how to live its life accordingly, and understand the ways of thriving, adapting, and surviving amidst the perpetual evolutions of search engines, Google in particular.

GOOGLE: AN OVERVIEW

Primarily, Google, Inc. works under two umbrellas—Mobile and Google: The Mobile Section cover the mobile devices and apps venture it had acquired from Motorola. The Google Section covers the fields of Search, Advertising, Operating Systems and Platforms, and Enterprise Products.

⌨ Search – encompasses a very broad index of online content and websites, made available by its search engine to anybody connected to the Internet

The bottom line is enhancing ways for people connecting to free information.

⌨ Advertising – covers the scopes of Google Local, Mobile, Display, AdSense, and AdWords Programs.

Google offers a wide range of tools and services for advertisers covering all scales, big and small— from plain and simple text ads to mobile advertising and display, and to publishers.

❖ Google Local – gives users pertinent information on localities that includes telephone phone numbers, street addresses, operating hours, directions and local inquiries such as landmarks, parks, businesses, restaurants, and shops directly on google.com and Google Maps for both desktop and mobile devices.

❖ Google Mobile Program – develops user-friendly ads products, helping advertisers for widening their reach, and publishing partners for delivering pertinent and helpful ads to users while on the go.

❖ Google Display Advertising Program – constitutes the images, text, videos, and various interactive ads running across the Web on both desktop and smart mobile media, as well as handheld gadgets like tablets and net notebooks.

❖ Google AdWords Program – presents ads, which are pertinent and helpful to search inquiries.

❖ Google AdSense Program – render websites of the Google network to present ads.

💻 Operating Systems and Platforms – include Google Chrome Operating System (OS) and the Google Books, TV, and Android platforms (combining certain computers and operating systems).

❖Google Chrome Operating System (OS) – is an open source operating system and having Google Chrome Web Browsing System as its cornerstone. The creation of both systems revolves around the central 'S-doctrines' of security, simplicity, and speed.

❖ Google Books Platform – designed to help users search, discover, and digest contents of printed books online.

❖ Google TV Platform – provides users the experience of searching content for watching television and surfing the Internet, all on a single monitor or screen.

❖ Android Platform – is free, and fully opened source mobile software applicable to developers for creating various applications for mobile phone and tablet devices.

💻 Enterprise Products – offer user-friendly Google technologies and various hardware products for business and industrial set-ups.

FOCUSING ON USER EXPERIENCE

Ever since Lawrence E. Page and Sergey Brin founded Google in 1998, Search has truly made a considerable progress and improvement.

However, the company's primordial objective remains the same and steadfast— continuously developing and evolving Search towards improving, for always, the usefulness of results and user experiences, as well as meeting all the discriminating expectations of users worldwide.

In the last year alone, Google launched close to 1,700 initiatives for improvements and innovations to Search! Starting from innovations, as the Knowledge Graph, to search updates, to its ranking algorithms, Google ensured aligning with their objective the continuance of highlighting authoritative and relevant contents.

Google's mission is organizing all the information in the world and establishing it universally to be useful and accessible to everybody. This goes hand in hand with their goal of ever providing users with the most relevant and useful information.

The way Google generates improvements or modifications to its search algorithm in order to meet their goal undergo the following processes:

❖ Quality Testing for Search Evaluators
❖ Parallel Experimentations and Metrics Analyses
❖ Actual Traffic Experiments or Live User Tests

❖ Launch

Every possible notion and proposed modification to Search undergoes rigid user testing and assessment processes for analyzing specific metrics. Whenever the examination demonstrates a change that carries only less useful results, Google will never launch such a proposed improvement.

Any modifications Google perform to Search always hinge upon its goals and mission. For that reason, the company never accepts any form of payments from anybody for their site's inclusion in search results.

Instead, Google only sells advertising, and never Search results. Google had always believed about the significance of the free and useful information that should be accessible to everyone. Thus, Ads actually render Google to offer a free search engine, which functions just as well for everyone.

Ads sometimes appear in your search results upon using Google Search. Yet, for all you know, Google practices the value of transparency by distinguishing between organic and paid results, labeling clearly the ads so you could easily recognize them in the entire search page. (Refer to Image-1.) It only displays ads whenever they are pertinent to the search you make.

As responsible as Google can be, it only charges the advertisers soon after the users begin interacting with their ads. As it is always the case, Google's interest always boils down to displaying only useful results, including useful ads. Fact is that Google only run ads so seldom to avoid annoying users in their Search experience.

Lest misconstrued again, Google's financial ties with commercial entities do not influence its changes in Search algorithms. In the same way, partner advertisers never receive any special favors in deciding search requests or organic search concerns.

Therefore, Google only ensures handling all these search concerns based upon impact and significance to users, and never because of commercial links with the company.

EMPOWERING WEBSITE CREATORS / OWNERS

Google has been largely responsible for determining the online existence or presence of both businesses and publications, including your site. It provides you with extensive communication channels, tips, and troubleshooting tools to help you and other website creators and owners alike to understand the ways and functionalities of Search; and thereby, manage optimally your Search visibility. Among the bulk of Google's assistance are:

💻 Website Support Documentations and Informative Resources – The Google Webmaster Central Portal (www.google.com/webmasters/) offers a convenient one-stop interactive shop for your website requirements on support documentation.

The assistance extends to furnishing informative resources, particularly through starter guides and over a thousand instructional videos contained in the YouTube channel of Google Webmaster Help (www.youtube.com/GoogleWebmasterHelp/).

🖥 Live Support and Expert Advice – As a site owner, you can avail all the help you may need concerning your site from vastly experienced webmasters or even learn from Google workers at the Google Webmaster Forum (www.productforums.google.com/forum/).

🖥 Website Troubleshooting Tools – Google's Search Console tool (www.google.com/webmasters/tools/) helps you troubleshooting your site by:

❖ Getting alerts for critical issues or displaying errors found on your site, and advising you how to fix them,

❖ Diagnosing for malware and other programs with undesirable or harmful effects,

❖ Evaluating readabilities of your content and site metrics,

❖ Analyzing clicks from Google Search to see how your traffic alters over time, where your traffic comes from, and what search entries will most probably show up on your site. Additionally, the tool enables you to see which of your pages have the lowest and highest click-through rates from the search results.

❖ With the Mobile-Friendly Test, you will know which queries are coming from smartphones so you can capitalize such information towards improving your mobile optimization and target base.

❖ With the <u>PageSpeed Insights</u>, you will be able to reduce page-loading times and improve user experiences on your site.

Indeed, with all these tools and communication assistance, Google empowers you to build a Search-friendly site for users, and at the same time, showing up well in Search results.

Besides continuously sharing helpful information about how Search functions, Google also responsibly keeps on trying to place the proper balance of maintaining the World Wide Web to be as safe and as useful as it can be by promoting as well safe sound, and useful websites and SEO practices.

As a result, Google invests heavily in structuring quality algorithms along with manual reviews for ensuring sites (usually, spam sites) shall never surge rising at the top of SERPs through manipulative and deceptive means.

Such an investment is very important to upright users and responsive websites because most of these spam sites mislead users or effect serious damage, which may even lead to breaches in website security.

Battling against spam for maintaining a safe and useful Web has always been an arduous challenge for Google along the course of meeting its goals.

While it really wants to be very transparent as much as possible regarding how Search works, Google has also been too cautious not to disclose too many details of its algorithms that would enable irresponsible users to degrade the user experience by tricking the search results.

For this reason, gone are the days of the most notorious black hat SEO practices like keyword stuffing and links purchasing that pass the previous PageRank algorithm (named after the Google founder) or sneaking onto the page invisible texts.

Although many confirm that PageRank sculpting has now been outdated, Google is still actually using it but has no longer revealed its detailed information of its enhanced and much-tightened version of their PageRank algorithm.

Nowadays, Google has been trying to resolve an uptrend of hacking on several legitimate websites, many of them encountering deceptive and manipulative display ads redirecting their clueless users to unrelated and impertinent sites.

BASIC PRINCIPLES OF GOOGLE SEARCH

Google has clearly set out its Quality Webmaster Guidelines (www.support.google.com/webmasters/), which specifically call out manipulative and deceptive site behaviors for their automatic demotion/removal.

Nevertheless, the guidelines also provide distinct processes of restrictions and qualifications or

<u>reconsiderations for appeals soon as addressing the violations and sanctions.</u>

To guide you further towards your ideal white hat SEO 2017 / 2018 practices, Google's fundamental principles hinge upon the following:

🖥 Create pages intended primarily for users, and never for search engines.

🖥 Never deceive or trick your users.

🖥 Avoid manipulations, deceptions, and trickeries for improving your search engine rankings. Better, use these rules of thumb; ask yourself:

❖ Whether you would feel at ease explaining to a Google worker or a website competitor what you have done.

❖ Whether what you have done will help your users.

❖ If search engines never existed, would you have done what you did?

🖥 Create an engaging, unique, and valuable website, and make it stand out in your niche.

Furthermore, guide yourself with these specific guidelines for avoiding the following techniques:

🖥 Abusing markups for rich snippets (creating empty pages just to possess structured data)

💻 Auto-generated content (consisting of random nonsensical text filled with search keywords)

💻 Cloaking (providing different results than expected)

💻 Creating pages bearing malicious behaviors, like phishing, and installed viruses or other malware

💻 Creating pages with fewer contents and without originality

💻 Doorway pages (generating multiple pages— through keywords proximate to hierarchal search results or substantial domain names— just to funnel users to a single relevant page)

💻 Engaging in notorious link schemes

💻 Forwarding automated queries and other types of auto-access to Google without prior notice (asking for rank checking)

💻 Hidden text or links (usually keyword-rich, by applying white text over a white background, situating texts behind images, employing cascading style sheets (CSS) for off-screen text positioning, setting to o-font size, and linking a minute character such as a dash in the middle of a content)

💻 Joining 'thin' affiliate programs that do not provide benefits to users since most contents are duplicates of the original merchants

🖥 Loading pages with impertinent keywords

🖥 Scraped contents (filling up pages with copied, modified, republished, reproduced, or embedded multimedia contents from other sites)

🖥 Sneaky redirects (redirecting users to a different URL other than initially requested)

Instead, just adhere following these basic website management ideal practices:

🖥 Checking and keeping track of your site for hacking, and taking away immediately the hacked content as soon as it appears.

🖥 Preventing spam generated by users on your site, and removing it immediately upon its appearance.

INCREASING ACCESSIBILITY TO FREE INFORMATION

🖥 Strong Commitment to a Free and Open Web – Since Google always believed in providing open access to free information, it tries so hard making all the information from the Web available to all users, regardless of one's educational attainment or economic status in life.

This belief stems from the notion that society only works best when it reserves a space to accommodate and hear all voices.

Therefore, Google serves best its users for having infinite access to an unfathomable coverage of greatly diverse contents coming from a mélange of sources.

This is the main reason why Google does not delete contents from its search results, except, of course, in restricted instances such as a violation of Google's <u>Quality Webmaster Guidelines</u>, obliging to legal removals, or yielding to the request of a webmaster accountable for the content.

⌨ Search Results Reflect Upon Published Web Contents – Some Web contents may contain prejudices, offensive materials, and negative conventional or societal practices, perceptions, and attitudes.

There are possibilities that you may see such contents reflected in your search results, especially if your search requests match closely to certain languages used on these sites.

These controversial contents and sites do not reflect Google's preferences and opinions, but their continued presence on the Web rather reflects Google's belief in open access to free information. Meaning, Google does not delete links to such contents merely because they contain information or perspectives, for which a huge part of society may disagree.

⌨ Continuous Developments and Improvements for Search – Although it is considered inevitable for newer black hat SEO endeavors to exist, Google works tirelessly to thwart all these unfair practices and prevent irrelevant or poor quality contents appearing in search results.

In addition, the Web grows and changes steadily with its underlying contents not to mention the hundreds of fresh web pages published at each second.

Accordingly, Google finds incessantly smart and feasible algorithmic solutions, which are able to address concerns not only for a single search result page but also for thousands, if not, millions.

In summary, Google only wants to keep its patrons safe and enjoy the experiences of Search while respecting the cultural conventions and laws of approximately 200 countries where it offers its services.

How Google Search Engine Works

Negating the search engines, fresh web contents would never be accessible to the public. For great multitudes of people, Google has been synonymous with the Internet and has become the jumping-off point for searching new sites.

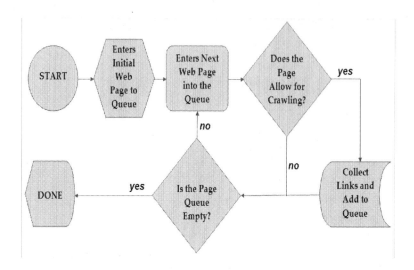

Image-9: Flowchart of How Search Engines Work

How Google and every principal search engine (Yahoo, Bing, and ask.com) works, undergoes three major essential functions:

⌨ Crawling – the discovery of a website and acquisition processes of its data

⌨ Indexing – the tracking and storing processes of crawled and organized data in a database

⌨ Retrieval and Ranking – the fetching up and returning process of relevant contents upon specific queries or requests by users on the search engine

CRAWLING

Before you even begin searching, Google is employing web crawlers, which gather data and information from across hundreds of billions of publicly available web pages and their contents for organizing them in the Google Search Index.

The process of crawling starts with a roster of website addresses culled from previous crawls and sitemaps furnished by website owners.

It involves combing and scanning the websites and collating their detailed data for each page such as titles, keywords, headings, linked pages, images, etc. Other web crawlers may also scan for various details, such as page layouts, the situation of links (crammed in, hidden, etc.), ads location on a page, etc.

When crawlers or bots intrude these websites, they activate a program (termed as, "spider," which can read several thousands of data per second) to visit pages upon pages as fast as possible.

The software uses the page links on those websites to discover and explore other pages. Meaning, any site linked from an indexed site will ultimately be crawled. Spiders, however, focus their attention on the newer websites, dead links, and certain editions or modifications of existing websites.

They determine which websites to crawl, and the frequencies and quantities of web pages to fetch from each website. Hence, some websites are crawled more often, while others are crawled more in-depth.

Nevertheless, a crawler may sometimes cease to continue crawling, especially when the page hierarchy or code structures of a web page are very complex.

Behind all these processes, Google's Website Troubleshooting Tools offer you and other website owners some meaty choices regarding how it would perform the crawling processes on your website:

💻 You may furnish detailed instructions about how to process certain pages on your site.

💻 You may request for a re-crawl of your URLs for re-indexing (using the Fetch as Google tool), especially when you made certain changes in a page of your site

💻 You may opt out altogether from the crawling process by excluding it using the robots.txt file.

Google denies any payments made to crawl more often a site. It only provides all sites with the same tools, ensuring the possible best results for all users.

INDEXING

As crawlers discover a webpage, the search engine's programming system depicts the content of the page, in the same manner, which a browser renders a page. The system takes note of all crawled data and vital criteria, and consequently, stores and keeps track of all this information in the Search index.

The Google Search Index composes more than a quadrillion of web pages and exceeds more than a million gigabytes in volume. It is similar to the index placed at the end of a book, but the only difference is that Google enters each word seen and contained on each web page indexed.

Thus, you could just imagine that the Search Index is a humongous scale of stored data— not only a room filled with books but seemingly the entire libraries in the world.

Actually, Google accumulates and organizes this gargantuan warehouse of knowledge in expansive storage data centers with hard memory drives reaching to thousands of petabytes (1,024 terabytes).

However daunting the indexing processes may be, Google continues to work beyond keyword matching through the Knowledge Graph— a knowledge-based or semantic-search data system, which puts together information, people, events, places, and all other stuff and topics people are more concerned about, to create an enhanced and interconnected search results that are more precise and relevant.

To accomplish such systemic data accumulation, Google not only organize data and information about web pages, but also various types of information such as searching easily for, texts and passages from billions of books from principal libraries, travel times from various local public transit agencies, or even facts from public sources like the UN or World Bank.

RETRIEVAL AND RANKING

The retrieval and ranking processes are where most search engines differ to one another. Each uses different criteria for their retrieval methods of picking up and choosing which pages suit best to return or display with what users requested or wanted to find.

It is no wonder why search results distinctively vary among the major search engines. For instance, the thesaurus-like search base of the Wolfram | Alpha computational knowledge search engine is uniquely different from Google's usage of its Knowledge Graph for search information.

The algorithms for ranking are responsible for checking and determining the relevance of each search query of users against billions of web pages indexed. Due to their complexities, search engine companies secure their ranking algorithms as their patented and exclusive industry secrets.

No SEO practitioner or digital content marketer can predict precisely whatever future ranking algorithm updates will be appearing. Even a number of Google workers are clueless about everything occurring or in Google— the most dominant search engine.

The only clear understanding users gained is that a better ranking algorithm always translates towards an effective and efficient search and user experience.

Of course, it is still always possible to exploit or manipulate search engines, but it is never so easy anymore.

Originally, search engines used the PageRank algorithm to rank sites by how frequent keywords appeared on a web page. This only resulted in the deceptive practice of keyword stuffing (richly filling pages with nonsensical keywords).

Still, using the same algorithm, the search engines emphasized subsequently the value of sites having several incoming links since they perceived the popularity of the site as relevant.

Just the same, this only compounded the abuses, which led to indiscriminate link purchasing / spamming around the entire Web.

At present times, mystery cloaks the ranking algorithms more than ever before. The previous and familiar SEO practices are no longer important. The rankings of search engine have now arisen from great user experiences and high-quality contents.

In addition, search engines have now already put more emphasis and bearing upon specific links, which depend highly upon the authoritative repute of the linking site. Fact is that search engines are now placing more value on links coming from a certain government agency rather than links stemming from link directories.

Thus far, after laying all these primary predicates, from the basic SEO practices to Google Search functionalities, you are now more than ready to confront the future of SEO 2017 | 2018, and react positively by devising your own strategies with respect to the parameters set by the search engines.

Of course, other factors affect towards shaping your strategies. As always, you only have to be prudent, patient, persevering, and responsible to accept change.

"Google only loves you when everyone else loves you first."
— **Wendy Piersall**, Professional speaker, entrepreneur, blogger

CHAPTER 4 – THE MOST EFFECTIVE STRATEGIES FOR SEO 2017 | 2018

"The future of SEO is here: understanding and marketing to specific and defined audiences through search engines."
— **Adam Audette**, Senior Vice President of Organic Search at Merkle

After learning about how Google Search and the ways its algorithms function— finding, ranking, and returning relevant results— it is now high time to outline the most effective and ideal SEO 2017 | 2018 strategies and techniques you should consider practicing at present.

The basis for forming these strategies comes from accumulated information on the latest research in the industry, as well as from the facts and significant insights laid out in the opening chapters of this book.

1 – EMPHASES ON MOBILE PAGE SEARCH AND BROWSING

Optimization practices for mobile devices have long been here and play a vital role in SEO for years. In fact, mobile and tablet devices had already overtaken desktop usage since the last quarter of 2016, when mobile phones and other similar handheld gadgets tallied about 51.3% of all the total Web browsing around the world. During this same period, Google introduced its Mobile-First Index.

For so long, Google had been crawling desktop editions of websites, making all this crawled data as its principal search engine index. Nevertheless, with the recent indexation update, Google has now begun using the mobile edition of a website as its primary search engine index.

This denotes Google will be deriving the creation and ranking of its search listings from the contents of mobile editions, including the current listings displayed to desktop users. Thus, it is truly necessary prioritizing your site's mobile version and content from this point onwards.

Google will be ranking both versions of your mobile and desktop website based upon signals received through the crawling processes on your site from a mobile perspective. Hence, how fast your page loads on your mobile website will be a prime determining factor in the rankings of both your mobile and desktop websites in Google.

Additionally, Google will certainly be looking at your mobile site's title, headings, generated contents, and structured data markups. Consequently, it will also use all these crawled data over the data from your desktop site.

In one of their blog posts, Google has declared, *"Our search index continues to be a single index of websites and apps; our algorithms will eventually use the mobile version of a website's content primarily to rank pages from that site."*

As for the full blast implementation of the mobile-first index, Google has yet to reveal a definite date since everything is still under experimentation, and ironing out a few more details to test users. If all goes well, then it could be sooner. If not, then Google might just push it back.

However, Google assured to thrust this forward in due time to more searchers upon becoming more at ease and confident with the mobile-indexation update.

Generally, many will benefit from such a promotion, particularly e-commerce websites. Shifting the focus to the promotion of mobile search only means ensuring businesses to have a much wider reach aside from their current desktop audience.

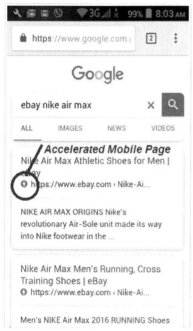

Image-10: Screen Capture of a Mobile Search Returning an Accelerated Mobile Page of an Ecommerce Site

Nonetheless, you should never underrate the value and potentials of enabling the desktop website to be more mobile-friendly. Always keep an eye on Accelerated

SEO 2018

Mobile Pages (AMP) to assure a higher traffic volume to your site.

Therefore, as early as now, you can now make your bright SEO moves and strategies like the following suggestions:

⌨ Create a mobile edition of your site's desktop version with any feasible formatting that is adaptive, responsive, and using the latest web technologies or progressive web applications (PWA). Take note, only a few articles of news sites have a mobile version existing as of now.

⌨ Construct the presentation of the web pages and contents both in desktop and mobile versions to be similar. Otherwise, you will be at a loss in the rankings. Bear in mind that a desktop search discards some of the pages and visible content in a mobile version.

Thus, when the mobile-first index goes full swing, your mobile version will surely lose its SEO visibility. As a resolve, Google highly suggests quick responsiveness of your mobile site to avoid this issue.

⌨ Implement structured data markups in your mobile version. Some will most likely neglect this suggestion due to focusing more emphasis on optimizing speed and responsiveness. Besides, the mobile-first index does not usually implement the schema markup.

No matter what, Google urgently requires such fundamental markup information! In addition, Google really campaigns on promoting rich cards used for mobile search that somehow duplicate the strategy of giving incentives practiced previously with rich snippets.

Sometimes, we may think about this as the main reason why Google insisted firmly on applying to the structured data a lightweight linked data format as JavaScript Object Notation for Linked Data (JSON-LD)— a technique to encode linked data using JSON.

Anyway, if your performance worries you, then it would be the proper time adopting JSON-LD since it only necessitates fewer efforts for you to convert your current JSON markups to JSON-LD.

🖥 Rethink your optimizations for conversion and user experience for mobile and desktop versions. For example, Google's demotion on tabbed contents lately has led many websites to start getting rid of all their tabs, and rather presenting their contents immediately. Such limitation will no longer apply soon as mobile-first index arises.

🖥 Plan and recreate a newer link building strategy for having a separate mobile website. This is, however, a defensive strategy since everything is still vague as to what happens about inbound links to desktop editions in a world of mobile-first indexing.

Probably, hopefully, and eventually, Google may happen to find means of making the link graph algorithm independent from the nature of websites.

2 – Undertake Intentional Link Building

Ever since Search began, links have already been a vital impetus for higher rankings of websites. In fact, Google and several other SEO studies confirmed that links as being among the top troika of ranking factors, together with content and effective communication or RankBrain.

Truly, the potentials of links are so powerful that they go beyond our imaginations. However, links per se are never sufficient to redeem or save low-quality contents.

Links can only spell the big difference if your content is competent and relevant. As Matt Cutts used to say, *"The objective is not making your links appear natural; but that, your links ARE natural."*

Just the same, you can always gain easily high traffic volume through performing white hat SEO link building, where you may contact other site owners and request linking their relevant contents and sites to yours.

3 – Optimization for Voice Search

The 2016 Internet Trends, as reported by the renowned Silicon Valley venture capital firm, Kleiner Perkins Caufield & Byers, stated that requests and queries for voice search have undergone an increase 35 times since 2008, and keep on growing steadily since then.

Furthermore, the report cited that speech recognition accuracy records an almost perfect 95% rate, and it will only be a matter of time to hit 99%, which could really be a game changer. Whatever the case may be, voice search is seemingly the next great frontier of Search.

For one, a current trend that could apparently become the new normal sooner than soon due to voice search is the long and wordy search queries. Thus, prepare your site for optimizing your mobile site contents for voice search. The following parameters will help you in your voice search optimization goals:

🖥 Know what search engine are you optimizing for voice search; is it on Google Now, Apple's Siri, or Microsoft Bing's Cortana virtual voice assistants?

🖥 Understand how users apply voice search.

🖥 Get used to being mobile–friendly as Google shifts its primary indexing towards a mobile world.

4 – IMPROVEMENT ON FEATURED SNIPPETS

A 2015 study showed that about 20% of all search queries in the world resulted to display rich answers. SEO analysts then figured out this number would significantly be much higher in 2017-2018.

Thus, it would be vital for you to optimize intentionally search requests of your site; more so, if you intend your content displayed for common niche-related queries. You can fulfill this through a number of ways.

For more guidance on improving chances for featuring your snippets, refer to the Meta-innovations on <u>using rich snippets</u>.

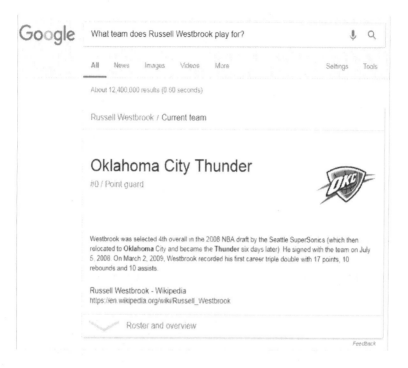

Image-11: Sample Search Return Display of Rich Answers from a Certain Search Query

5 – DEVELOPMENT OF LOCAL SEARCH

The concept of engaging with marketing locally with the use of mobile is more urgent and brighter. The relevance and importance of local search are even greater, with mobile becoming the primary search traffic source coupled with the unbeatable successes of chat-bots and virtual personal assistants.

This has been so, despite some innovative technologies, like those mobile-connected iBeacons, which could hardly reign in the market, probably because the iBeacon technology seems extremely advanced in relation to consumer behaviors.

Local search via mobile would really seem to be the strategic ground why Google updated the Possum algorithm and the ubiquitous tests in local you currently notice. Moreover, it is also perhaps a technical reason why Google acquired last year the Silicon Valley-based data analytics startup, Urban Engines, which uses data to provide insights into cities and how the populace move around in these locales.

Therefore, it is imperative optimizing for local search nowadays, especially if your business entails a local component. You must work on getting your site visible and found easily for local keyword entries, as the bulk of your future customers will be turning to their mobiles searching for local businesses, information, and products.

6 – REFINEMENT OF THE USER EXPERIENCE: INCREASING THE CLICK-THROUGH RATES (CTR)

A good and sustainable digital marketing campaign takes notes on some important factors, which you actually test by asking yourself: Does the interface on your site satisfy your customers, visitors, and users? Do they face troubles or incur any issues while placing an order, making a purchase, signing up, or simply navigating your site?

Alternatively, you may conduct a series of A-B test experiments and surveys to find out what they do not want to see, what they are searching for, and what works for them.

Whatever you wish to promote, or whenever your site satisfies the needs and wants of the users, they are able to get as many benefits as they can out of the information you presented, and even suggest your site to others. Consequently, this increases the volume of traffic to your site.

Throughout the years, providing an excellent user experience directly plays a vital role in site rankings. Nevertheless, what has always been an indirect influence to boost site rankings is the connection between the site and the metrics of user experience (bounce rates, net promoter score (NPS), click-through rates, etc.).

However, recent research shows an existence of a direct link between higher rankings and trouncing the anticipated CTR of other pages in the SERPs. Otherwise stated, if your content becomes visible in the SERPs, yet, it never outperforms the other pages in relation to clicks, then you may not be able to hold any longer onto your rankings.

As a resolve, optimizing your meta-data for your selected keywords will be one of the most significant steps you may take for ensuring to retain stronger CTR. Note that your meta-description and title tag serve as your advertising copy in the SERPs, enticing to engage viewers and clicking through.

7 – Growing Up with Natural Language Understanding (NLU): Research on Relative Keywords

By default, every aspect of Google Search is now using machine learning processes and artificial intelligence (AI) systems since AI expert, John Giannandrea, took the helm of Google Search as Senior Vice President of engineering last year.

Hence, SEO 2017 | 2018 will be anticipating more about the usage of artificial intelligence and machine learning, and perhaps, expecting certain modifications for improving the Hummingbird algorithm at every stage.

As proof of this, Google is fixated on interpreting semantics and processing of natural language. Giannandrea affirms, saying, *"Understanding language is the sought-after objective of machine learning,"* and further discussed, *"and the latest research concerns of Google's Natural Language Understanding (NLU) group include multilingual modeling, syntax, conversation, discourse, question answering, sentiment analysis, summarization, and building typically enhanced learners applying unlabeled and labeled data, indirect supervision, and state-of-the-art modeling."*

The reason why Google embraces irresistibly such deep interests in contextual and natural language is that Google only wants to provide the best answers and results to the Search needs and requests of users. Thus, in order to accomplish this objective, Google should:

🖥 Understand the content of each web page document, fulfilling aims of interpreting semantics.

🖥 Understand what Search users are actually trying to search for— through using either, their voice or typing manually requests in the search box, fulfilling aims of natural language processing.

🖥 Allowing users to be mobile, and that, they really need not be at their desks to require answers, fulfilling aims of mobile indexing and open accessibility to information.

To grow up with natural language understanding, we always go back to keyword research. Although it is among the simplest form and essentially fundamental to digital marketing, keyword research still holds much importance in every aspect of SEO.

However, keyword research shall never be about merely finding one or a couple of words or phrases, and applying them to your content. Ideally, you should think and search for phrases that connect contextually or semantically to your subject theme or topic. For example, when blogging about playing chess, you will most likely need using words such as, 'opening,' middle game,' 'endgame,' 'castling,' 'en passant,' 'draw,' and 'checkmate.'

Applying these words is proving to Google that you are covering comprehensively your topic. Moreover, it would mean that you have a more detailed and balanced article, which benefits the user experience.

An excellent tool for this is RankBrain, which focuses primarily towards helping refine search queries processed by Google. However, Google also confirms that it also uses the system for ranking web pages, as one of its prime triumvirate ranking factors along with content and links.

Aside from RankBrain, newer sets of keyword tools, which create source word and keyword groups, can also help you more effectively for using both targeted and complementary keywords in your site's contents.

8 – ENHANCEMENT OF THE CONTENT MARKETING PLAN

A proper and unique content marketing plan is definitely essential to build influence and entice high traffic volume, as well as having greater chances of besting your competitors fond of imitating. Planning should actually focus on two main aspects, with care and caution:

🖳 Writing Longer Content – At the average, ranking at the top in most of the searches involves writing articles containing a total word count of not less than 2,000. Nevertheless, it is noteworthy that it is not just all about the rambling length of the content that augments a boost in rankings, but also, the quality of the content.

Virtually all studies conducted through theses years demonstrated clear correlations between higher rankings and lengthy contents. These studies even suggested minimum word counts from 1,200-1,500.

As a rule of thumb when aiming to rank your content, write a minimum word count of 1,200 for regular blog posts while 2,000+ words for contents that will surely remain perennially fresh, interesting, or well-liked.

⌨ Pursuing High Topical Authority (Comprehensive Content) – Studies also showed that comprehensive and lengthy contents, albeit, not using any specific keywords at all, widely surpassed in rank those brief and shallow contents optimized for certain keywords.

In other words, the focus is more on the breadth (comprehensiveness) and depth (quality) of the content instead of attaining word count and injecting keywords. Undoubtedly, such contents are better for the user experience, and in turn, convert to higher rankings.

9 – CONSIDERING PERSONALIZATION AS SEO STRATEGY

Another main feature of Google is personalized search, which is a result of enhanced context and search entities based on user behavior and social preferences. Hence, in terms of considering personal assistants in mobile, personalization would really seem to be very important.

Personalization denotes that Google will be auto-suggesting and present more frequently contents from pages that are already in your search history or via search entities linked from sites already existing in your search history, or resultant contents relevant to your country or locality.

Meaning, on one hand, focusing on a shorter and strategic level, targeting long-tail queries is necessarily important. On the other hand, focusing on a longer and tactical extent, it would be much more significant rendering your brand or site context synonymous with your products or services. You can achieve this easily by focusing primarily high up the search funnel with the right content and having the right format, and then, publish it at the right time and promote it to the right users, visitors, and consumers.

10 – SPEEDING UP THE WEBSITE AND OVERALL PERFORMANCE

Ever since the introduction of Search, Google has emphasized the urgency of having fast websites. With the advent of the mobile-first index, site speed will certainly be an essential ranking factor in SEO 2017 | 2018.

In Google's latest study, *'The Need for Mobile Speed,'* it found out that the abandonment rate of visiting mobile sites ran to about 53% when their pages take longer than 3 seconds to load. This prompted Google to re-emphasize the importance of site speed. If you are unsure of how fast your mobile site loads, find it out by checking your site with Google's Mobile-Friendly Test and PageSpeed Insights tools. However, you may also apply plug-ins and other tested techniques for immediate resolutions of increasing your site speed.

⌨ PageSpeed Insights Tool – evaluates a web page performance for both desktop and mobile devices, and how the page can improve further on its performances concerning:

❖ Above The Fold Loading Time – Elapsed time between the instances a user searches a new page and the browser renders the 'above-the-fold' content.

❖ Full-Page Loading Time – Elapsed time between the instances a user searches a new page and the browser renders fully the page.

Additionally, the tool checks or detects whether a page was able to apply the best practices for the device's usual performances. Refer to Images-12A and 12B for the issues of site speed and usability rules with their corresponding resolutions.

Nevertheless, since performances of network connection vary substantially, PageSpeed Insights just considers page performance aspects, which are independent of network connections such as, the configuration of the server, a page's HTML structure and the application of external resources like images, and CSS, JavaScript, and images.

🖥 Mobile-Friendly Test Tool – is a quick and easy way for testing how mobile-friendly is a page. The results of the tests usually include screenshots of how the page displays and appears to Google using a mobile device. It also provides a list of whatever mobile usability issues it finds on the page and site.The following table, which lists the common performance best practices for site speed and usability, helps to guide you further in optimizing your mobile and desktop site versions.

COMMON PERFORMANCE BEST PRACTICES	
SITE SPEED RULES	**RESOLUTIONS** [*Recommendations and / or References to Google's Quality Webmaster Guidelines (GQWG)*]
🖥 **Avoid Landing Page Redirects**, *or the multiple additional HTTP request-response cycles or roundtrips that delay page renderings*	*Refer to* **Redirects and User-Agent Detection** *at* GQWG
🖥 **Enable GZIP Compression** *for all HTTP requests*	*Refer to* **Text Compression with GZIP** *at* GQWG; *or, configure the browser to recommended settings based from the sample configuration files from the* **HTML5 Boilerplate**
🖥 **Improve Server Response Time**, *or reduce server response time under 200 milliseconds*	*Consult the documentation for performance optimization best practices of your website framework or content management platform*
🖥 **Leverage Browser Caching**, *or specify an explicit caching policy*	*Refer to* **Caching with Cache-Control** *and* **Validating Cached Responses With eTags** *at* GQWG

🖥 **Minify Resources**, *or remove unnecessary or redundant data without affecting how the browser processes the resources (i.e., code comments and formatting, removing unused code, using shorter variable /function names, etc.)*	*Minify your HTML, CSS, and JavaScript resources:* ❖ *To minify HTML, try* **HTML Minifier** ❖ *To minify CSS, try* **CSSNano** *and* **CSSO** ❖ *To minify JavaScript, try* **UglifyJS**; *also try the equally effective* **Closure Compiler**
🖥 **Optimize Images**, *or analyze image metrics for optimization such as, type of data encoded, image format capabilities, quality settings, resolution, etc.*	*Use tools such as the* **Convert Binary** *created by ImageMagick for optimizing images*
🖥 **Optimize CSS Delivery**, *or unblock rendering of external style sheets*	*Refer to* **Render-Tree Construction, Layout, And Paint** *and* **Render Blocking CSS**
🖥 **Prioritize Visible Content**, *or reduce the size of the above-the-fold content to a minimum compression of 14.6kB*	*Limit the size of the data (HTML markup, images, CSS, JavaScript) needed to render the above-the-fold content of the page by either:* ❖ *Structuring the HTML to load first the critical above-the-fold content* ❖ *Reducing the amount of data used by the page's resources*

Image-12A: Common Performance Best Practices on Site Speed and Usability Rules

SEO 2018

💻 **Remove Render-Blocking JavaScript**, *or analyze how JavaScript affects the critical rendering path, whether a blocking external JavaScript file exists in the above-the-fold portion*	*Refer to* **Adding Interactivity with JavaScript** *at* GQWG
💻 **Use Asynchronous Scripts**, *to enable downloading a script in the background before the page renders completely*	*Ensure using the asynchronous version of scripts such as the popular scripts of Twitter, Google+, ShareThis, Facebook, StumbleUpon, etc., which all supports asynchronous script loading*
SITE USABILITY RULES	**RESOLUTIONS** *[Recommendations and / or References to Google's Quality Webmaster Guidelines (GQWG)]*
💻 **Configure The Viewport**, *or specify a viewport that adapt to different mobile or handheld devices*	*Optimize pages to display well on mobile and handheld devices by including a meta viewport in the head of the document specifying the formula,* <meta name=viewport content="width=device-width, initial-scale=1">, *or perform* **Viewport Documentation from Opera and Mozilla, Creating a Mobile-First Responsive Web Design from HTML5 Rocks**, *or* **Configuring the Viewport in the Safari Web Content Guide**

💻 **Size Tap Targets Appropriately**, *or prevent users from being frustrated hitting accidentally tap targets (i.e., buttons, links, or form fields)*	*Ensure the most important tap targets on site (those that users most frequently use) to be larger enough, at least 7mm on mobile, or 48 CSS pixels; or, ensure extra spacing between smaller tap targets, with no other tap targets within 5mm on mobile, or 32 CSS pixels, both horizontally and vertically*
💻 **Avoid Plugins** *on mobile devices since they do not support special types of web content like, Flash, Silverlight, and Java*	*Create using native Web technologies, including content requiring first-class support for audio and video, advanced graphics and presentation effects, network connections, local storage, and file access to ensure accessibility of rich contents on all devices*
💻 **Size Content To Viewport**, *so the page content fits horizontally within the specified viewport size, thus, no longer necessitating the user to pan horizontally to view all the content*	*Configure the viewport so that pages render correctly on several devices. Avoid setting large absolute CSS widths for page elements and large absolute positioning values that cause elements falling outside the viewport on small screens. Rather use relative width values such as, width: 100%*
💻 **Use Legible Font Sizes**, *prior to scaling down to mobile devices*	*Configure a viewport to ensure scaled fonts as displayed across various devices. Use a base font size of 16 CSS pixels. For vertical space requirements between characters, use the browser default line-height of 1.2-em*

11 – LINKING TO VIDEO AND IMAGE SEARCH

Although it has not stolen time from watching TV, patronizing video online has been growing steadily; and studies show that desktop and laptop are still the devices most used to access video online, although smartphones are quickly on the rise.

In more concrete terms with relation to digital marketing strategy and SEO 2017 | 2018, video search has become a channel to widen the reach of information, with which any SEO practitioner would consider and explore more seriously than before.

Even in terms of digital public relations, SEO should begin considering as much online video celebrities and influencers as any authoritative bloggers. Videos nowadays are akin to contents where they can generate useful links to websites.

From another point of view, image search has now become Google's old-fashioned thing, unwilling or unable to change and adapt. For most SEO practitioners, image search has not been much of help in bringing traffic to sites throughout the years. On the side of Google, image search has never been quite profitable.

Perhaps, this has been among the reasons why Google purchased the startup Paris-based Moodstocks and invested heavily in machine learning and artificial intelligence technology to support the innovative smartphone features of image recognition.

Nowadays, more people engage in showrooming, which is actually looking at a certain product in a physical store, taking photos of the product using their smartphone, and thereafter, searching and purchasing such product online at a much cheaper price.

Apparently, with Google's reverse image search feature, Google practically helps people on such image searches due to image recognition. You can actually use an image as your search to look for related images all over the Web. Upon searching, your results can include, similar images, websites that include the searched image, and various sizes of the searched image.

Image search works ideally when the image will most probably show up in other destinations on the Web. Hence, you will be getting more results for popular landmarks, food recipes, and other most commonly searched photos than you do with personal images.

Moreover, using www.schema.org/Product, you can tag the photos of your products in order for Google to pair product images easily to other aspects such as stock availability, promotional offers, and prices.

Having this data, it could begin monetizing or converting the images as legal tenders in a hierarchal order. Additionally, image links and search can help you receive more traffic to your site. Alt-tagged images add content that can be crawled on your page, not to mention enhancing your user experiences.

With further acquisitions of EyeFluence, (eye-tracking interface for augmented reality (AR), virtual reality (VR), and mixed reality (MR)), Anvato (platform for video encoding, editing, publishing, and distributing on both Web and mobile), and Famebit (platform for marketers collaborating with video creators to endorse on social media sites), it implies that video/images search are the focal points for Google.

12 – VALUING USER INTENTS

With the updates of Google's algorithms, user intents nowadays underscore the switch towards user experience over optimizing exclusively on search engines. Although the idea of user intent has been around for a time, it is beginning to gain solid ground as a vital metric to focus on SEO, because user intent has the tendency to:

🖥 Relate What Users Look for – Upon assessing user intent, you should look beyond the more notable search terms, and begin understanding directly about what people are most commonly searching. You can achieve this by either using Google's AdWords Keyword Tool or HubSpot's Keywords Tool.

🖥 Provide Suggestions for Unique Keywords – Think and act more as a user rather than an SEO by capturing the most probable words users may input in the search field.

🖥 Help Design Better Landing Pages and Raise Conversions – When you understand what the needs and wants of the user, you can very well design landing pages for accommodating all their desires.

🖥 Emphasize Clearer Demographics – It would always be more lucrative and prudent catering to a specific location within the realms of local and mobile search. Keywords based on certain locations are clear denotations of what users are seeking. Having such type of demographic data makes it easier for you in designing your site's content, product marketing, and positioning, as well as public relations aligned with the information.

🖥 Produce Satisfactory Overall Content Strategies – Valuing user intents compels you to create contents resort to the specific interests, needs, and concerns of the users or audiences you are targeting.

EFFECTIVE SEO THAT WILL BECOME OBSOLETE: A PREDICTION FOR SEO 2017 | 2018

The rate of the changing algorithm updates on Google, behavioral patterns of new users, newer technologies, and newer means of searching the Web are all working in unison for keeping SEO professionals on their toes.

Why would not they be busy when each year ushers in the end of a bunch of erstwhile effective SEO practices while leaving only a few of the distinctively best SEO practices the same? The Panda 2011 and Penguin 2012 algorithms put an end to two principal SEO strategies— writing manipulative and keyword-stuffed on-page content and the mass acquisition of unreliable links, regardless of quality, from almost everywhere possible.

Yet, even minor strategic shakeups and less-intensive new impositions may lead to substantial impacts on the SEO community as a whole.

While approaching the yearend, here is a compilation of the currently effective SEO practices perceived by experts to be extinct by the end of the following year:

💻 Optimizations Focused on Keywords – For a while, page optimizations focused on keywords has been heading to an exit. Although keywords associated with your business niche found in the content and title is still somehow significant, keyword-focused strategies, in general, are now declining in importance.

Instead, the general focus shifts now to content marketing, especially for building a brand online. The Hummingbird algorithm update revolutionized the Search by introducing semantic searching. Meaning, the algorithm no longer considers keywords as much as it does with the metrics of user intents.

At present, with Google bolstering the Search through its RankBrain system, the semantic contexts and use of the natural language of search queries and requests will even grow further with significance.

Additionally, as the system maps strangely and in a more unpredictable fashion the various interpretations of ambiguous user search queries, even the application of long-tailed keyphrases, which had worked previously well for Hummingbird, may begin waning in relevance.

🖥 Exclusive Text Contents – While perennial studies had always indicated contents using multimedia perform better against written-only contents, content marketing techniques with exclusive text contents remain effective until now. However, with new features and platforms sprouting, coupled with the changing demographics online, the written-only content may be uncertain.

Definitely, the written content will always be here to stay. Nonetheless, if you are trying to stand out prominently in the crowd you really ought to infuse or spice up your written contents in the form of videos, images, and even audios, or possibly, elements that are more interactive. Besides, getting away with merely writing contents entails a stiffer competition.

🖥 Link Baiting thru Info-Graphics – It occurred in the recent past that info-graphics were the immediate keys to success, for as long as you include graphics alongside with data in a more perceptible way. Such a practice assured you of receiving hundreds of links the following day after posting.

With its surge in notoriety that resulted in oversaturation, link baiting via info-graphics is no longer much of the same level of success. While it is still very useful today, it can never guarantee success just like before.

Thus, to be successful receiving links through info-graphics, it necessitates you to stand out distinctively from the rest by creating truly exceptional pages on your site.

🖳 Link Building by the Bulk – This refers to the link building process of posting links to your site in forums, blogs, social media and social networking sites, and other channels that do not have any processes for an editorial review. Meaning, anyone can simply post anything at any time on these platforms.

With the recent Penguin algorithm update, along with a trending decline of performing this typical link building process, this practice is no longer very much effective. However, you may still use it for some measured benefits.

Today, websites already found the necessity and significance of having an editorial reviewing process or moderating their contents. In effect, these updates and revisions only compel more businesses towards pursuing link building by way of relationship building or goodwill, guest posting and publishing high-quality contents that entice receiving links on their own merit.

🖳 Optimizations for the Desktop Site Version – With the growing popularity in the use of mobile devices, where its traffic constantly outpaces that of desktops, Google is now more concern about providing sufficiently a great the mobile experience.

This only means to say that mobile optimization is posturing to become the norm and standard to appease mobile users. Therefore, as long as websites undergo sufficient optimizations for mobile, it will no longer matter sooner than later how sites appear on a desktop.

💻 Complete Focus on Google – During the last 15 years, search engine optimization has been synonymous with Google optimization. Such perceptions have good reasons after all since Google has undisputedly become the unequaled leader in the field of online search for the world's information, as it hosts the largest and most extensive user base.

Moreover, Google offers the most advanced technologies not only in Search but also, in online advertising, cloud computing and hardware/software applications. It also introduces almost all of the digital trends, directions, and features in Search, making it difficult for other the search engines catching up.

Nonetheless, this unanimous direction will be seeing a predictable shift ahead. Fact is that Google users are now beginning generating a declining trend in favor of other search engine platforms such as Yahoo! and Bing.

Even other startup versions of online search such as personal virtual digital assistants Cortana and Siri are now starting to reshape the dynamics of Search with user behaviors. Thus, it will no longer be sufficient to concentrate solely on search results generated by Google.

"SEO is never done. You cannot just 'SEO' your website and be done. It is a forever moving goal post."
— **Stoney deGeyter**, Author, speaker, and Web marketer

CHAPTER 5 – SEO DOMINATION IN GOOGLE SEARCH RESULTS

"Search engine optimization does not specialize in tasks that will make pigs soar high up in the sky. Its real task is to dig deeper into the genetics of a website and re-engineer the essential elements until it transforms into an eagle."
— **Bruce Clay**, Founder, and president of the global Internet marketing optimization firm, Bruce Clay, Inc.

After having an overview about the basics of SEO, Google's search engine fundamentals, how Search functions, as well as the effective strategies you can implement amidst the updates and revisions of Google's search engine, it is now high time outlining a concrete master plan, consisting of the essentials and rules guiding you dominating SEO 2017 | 2018 in Google search results.

However, prior to designing your plan, you must first have a good grasp on how to view SEO from the proper perspectives. For many SEO practitioners, they tend to find ways of doing the minimum of efforts working for the maximum initial return. Yet, in reality, it is extremely the opposite.

Apparently, SEO is among the best skills you can learn possibly and significantly in today's rapidly changing technologies. Succeeding with SEO only necessitates you working with greater efforts while receiving the least of returns. Truly, it is a slow, sore, sacrificing, yet, steady process; it is, after all, the ways and nature of succeeding.

In other words, Google does not trust you right from the start. That means you will not definitely rank on those moneymaking primary-page SERPs. You will surely be lost along the flow and mad rush among millions like you, who are all clawing and struggling their ways towards the top.

Therefore, trust is the real and foremost guiding principle of SEO. If you have the trust of Google, then you will rank consistently and highly. Otherwise, you will be lost in the unfathomable depths with the company of the lowest-ranking web pages!

ESSENTIAL TRUST COMPONENTS OF GOOGLE SEARCH

Learn that there is only a trio of components comprising Google's trust. For each component, several factors influence it. However, these factors are the essential building blocks of how the trust of Google functions.

As you would now consider trust as an integral part of Google's system and pursuits of relevancy, whatever you do must revolve around growing the trust of Google instead of losing it.

🖥 Indexed Age – Google gives great importance concerning the indexed age of your website and its contents. More often than not, a novel website in Google undergoes incurring a much harder time of ranking highly on its SERPs as opposed to a site with an indexed age.

Indexed age denotes the date when Google was able to discover the webpage or domain under consideration, and not upon the date for its initial release or registration.

🖳 Authority Profile – Google pursues seeing only an indicatively good and sound link profile signifying authority. These links imply quality links stemming from relevant, useful, and diverse contents coming from all over the Web.

Not only does Google care about the significance of websites linking to your domain, but also, it gives more importance to the quality and authority of the contents, where those links come from.

In addition, Google looks for Internet Protocol (IP)-diverse links; meaning, they should not all be originating from the same source. Furthermore, Google looks for a robust linking rate, whereby, the creation of high-quality links corresponds to an increased frequency along the course of time.

🖳 Underlying Content – Many SEO practitioners work hastily or carelessly, and deal with inadequately and superficially on content. They forget that the underlying content of a page is among the vital anchors tethering the page to Google's algorithms on relevancy.

As discussed, thin and spun contents containing errors and text duplicities can really be damaging. Thus, content must not only be lengthier, but also, highly engaging, well written, and keyword-focused.

Rules for Dominating SEO 2017 | 2018 in Google Search Results

Similar to anyone else, you possibly keep on wondering how your page can appear organically and relevantly on Google's SERPs. Whether you are practicing SEO in 2017, 2018, or any other year, it is significant paying homage to the trust components of Google search.

Nevertheless, there are actually a couple of hundreds of ranking factors attributed to Google's current algorithms. Yet, generally, there are three main fundamental rules you should be adhering to helping you dominate SEO 2017 | 2018 in Google search results.

Regardless of whatever changes Google imposes while moving forward, all these rules remain to provide the basic principles, which you should govern across your SEO activities to produce the greatest progress on capturing those lucrative and crucial SERPs. You only have to remember that nothing converts overnight; everything will take its time.

⌨ First Rule: Keep Working to Earn Google's Trust – Earning the trust of Google helps you succeed in SEO, and manifestations of this guiding principle continue to be evident in countless sites for years now.

However, several SEO people just simply overlook this guiding rule. The main question is how would one earn Google's trust?

Take for instance a real-world situation regarding the plight of a business startup that is about to open shop. Say, the new business is in dire need of fresh working capital, and the business owner goes into a bank to transact a loan with the bank manager.

As a new business, the enterprise will obviously face certain prejudices. Most likely, the bank denies granting the business a loan due to a lack of recognized records of accomplishments— a catch 22 in the making. For the business to jumpstart and grow, it would need capital; yet, receiving the capital requires the business to be in operation for a certain period of time, and consequently, merit proven histories of performance.

Such a situation incurring consequences that make it impossible to pursue an action is the same dilemma that will be confronting any newly established domain or website on the Internet. If Google had just discovered your site, regardless of when you first registered your domain name, it will surely be suspecting about your intents. In short, Google would not trust you; thus, your site would not land on the SERPs despite the ideal strategies you implement.

This has been a great obstacle occurring when entering SEO. However, there are methods to overcome the follies of the search engine, and most of these methodologies have something to do with those unscrupulous rule benders who keep tricking the system for the quick and easy money. Currently, Google knows all about these notorious schemes. You just have to keep on working to build its trust.

💻 Second Rule: Age Outdoes Beauty – More important than the beauty of your site is its age. Over time, Google always looks for consistency of your links.

How long should be the duration? It concerns years, actually. Despite building a site with an excellent link profile, a gorgeous appearance, a user-friendly interface, and faster loading pages, everything else would not matter without age.

Age refers to the indexed age of your website, its links, and contents. It is actually a combination of all these factors relating to age— what is the link velocity over time? What is the capacity of high-quality contents linking to your site, and the linking schedule?

Whether you are simply learning SEO of whatever year ahead for that matter, it is important to remember that the algorithms of Google are always on, evaluating and judging any sorts of behavior associated to your page, its links, contents, etc. If you perform a huge amount of work within a month or so, and subsequently abandon your site completely, all your efforts only go down the drain, and you just have to start all over again.

Everything just centers on both the indexed age of the site and freshness of content. Even if Google has just discovered your site within the last couple of years, and you still have not developed any healthy link profile, you would not still earn Google's trust. Bear in mind, the first rule is trust; but growing trust comes through with age.

⌨ Third Rule: Quality Outdoes Quantity All the Time —
Whatever you do on the Web, it is a firm and determined
rule that quality outdoes quantity every time. Never focus
on performing something several times. Instead, focus on
performing it the proper way within its required times.

For instance, never worry so much about pushing yourself
producing a number of contents daily; worry rather about
pushing yourself creating a good content weekly. That is
what Google all cares— quality.

When Google launched its Panda algorithm, it was actually
pursuing quality through user experience. More
significantly, it was simultaneously finding out poor quality
user experiences— navigating pages with the intents of
garnering only traffic and deceiving users through dubious
means to compel them purchasing a product or service via
affiliated links, if not, annoying them with an avalanche of
advertisements.

Google will neither appreciate nor tolerate such deceptive
practices since its aim is not only to enhance the overall
quality of its search engine but also, all the data and
information on the Web. It has devised and upgraded
cleverly all these rules and ranking factors to assure that
quality improves over time rather than deteriorates.

Thus, whatever SEO strategy you wish to apply, always
ensure that it is about creating quality and not quantity.
Exert time and efforts promoting quality over quantity.

Take note that user engagement levels count the most;
hence, the longer users stay in your site and spend reading

your content, the higher chances you will be gaining in terms of traffic, conversions, and higher rankings; but most importantly, the stronger signals of quality you will be relaying to Google. As Stoney deGeyter remarked, *"Search engine rankings are not actually the goal of SEO. They are a trophy of a job well done."*

"SEO fosters the natural, long-term growth of a website, and once you achieve its benefits, there is usually a ripple effect where you'll be getting traffic from sources other than search engines by means of other websites linking to yours. If you have the content or product that people want to see, it is only natural to attract inbound links."
— John I. Jerkovic

CHAPTER 6 – WEB ANALYTICS: TRACKING SEO PERFORMANCE

"Without the big data analytics, entities become blind, deaf, and mute, wandering out onto the Web like a lost deer on a freeway."
— **Geoffrey Moore**, Author, and consultant

Web analytics is a technical process of analyzing user behaviors to a website. In short, it is tracking your application of SEO strategies to fulfill a great user experience visiting on your site.

Essentially, using web analytics enables your business to entice more users, retain or lure more customers to your products or services, or to increase the spending power of your customers.

In addition, web analytics is oftentimes applicable as a component of customer relationship management (CRM) analytics. The overall website analyses may include the following:

🖥 Identifying probabilities of a given customer to re-purchase a product or service soon after purchasing it

🖥 Personalizing or customizing the site to regular visitors and customers

🖥 Monitoring the volume of expenditures made by each customer or any specific sets of stereotyped or profiled customers

🖥 Observing the locations or geographical areas, where the bulk and the minority of customers come from or visit the site, and buy specific products

🖥 Predicting products that customers will most and least likely purchase in the near future.

The goal is to push certain products or services to those customers that will most possibly buy them and to identify which products or services a particular customer will most likely purchase. Certainly, this helps increase ratios of revenue as to marketing expenditures.

Apart from all these useful features, web analytics can include tracking patterns of customer behaviors within the site in terms of the drill-down and click-through processes:

🖥 Drill-down —refers to clicking through a series of drop-down menus, or a hierarchy of files and folders in a graphical user interface. Hence, it allows users to react quickly to the desired action or functional unit.

🖥 Click-Through – also referred to as the click rate, is the number of clicks directed on an ad, and expressed as a percentage of the frequency of downloading the ad along with a page.

Both of these processes identify certain sites, from which customers arrive most of the time, and communicate with browsers to monitor and evaluate online behavior. Generally, web analytic results are in the form of graphs, tables, and charts.

GOOGLE ANALYTICS

Google has its own free and premium web analytics services— Google Analytics— and is currently the most widely applied among the web analytics services on the Internet. The service offers two versions:

🖳 Google Analytics 360, formerly Google Analytics Premium, which is a subscription-based service catering to business, industrial, and enterprise users

🖳 Google Analytics for Mobile Apps, a software development kit (SDK) that enables the gathering and analyzing of the usage data and information from Android Apps and iOS systems.

Google Analytics is user-friendly. All you have to do is sign up for your Google Analytics account; input the required info of the site you would like to monitor, after which, you will receive a tracking code, which you will paste on your monitored pages. This code lets Google know the visitations on your monitored site. Within just a few hours upon signing, you will be able to begin seeing the data on your site, as well as learning more about the various information of your audience.

Since the service has <u>Google AdWords</u> integrated into it, you are now able to review online promotions and campaigns by tracking the quality of the landing page, and conversions or goals. Goals could include lead generation, revenues, downloading specific files, and viewing certain pages.

For the regular users, the technical approach of Google Analytics is to present you a dashboard-type or at-a-glance view of the top-level data, and a more comprehensive data displayed further into the standard and custom reporting categories.

Analyses of Google Analytics can recognize quickly pages with poor performances using techniques like funnel visualization— determining where users came from (referrers, or HTTP header fields identifying the webpage address, i.e., URL or the internationalized resource identifier (IRI), which is an extension to the URL)— the duration of their stay in your site, and their geographical location.

It can also provide sophisticated features like visitor segmentation, where you can segment visitors in various set parameters such as per sessions, per hit levels, per revenues, per transactions, etc.

For e-commerce reporting, Google Analytics can track sales performances and activities. The e-commerce reports display your website's business transactions, sales revenues, and several other metrics related to commerce and your business.

With its Real-Time Analytics component, the service enables you to have insights in real-time about customers or visitors presently on-site.

Its Cohort Analysis feature helps you understand the behavioral patterns of component sets of users who are independent of your user population. This is beneficial, especially to analysts and marketers in implementing successfully their marketing strategies.

Most importantly, Google Analytics incorporates its Google Website Optimizer, which has undergone a rebranding to Google Analytics Content Experiments.

IMPORTANCE OF GOOGLE ANALYTICS TO SEO

Admittedly, through all these features, Google Analytics greatly helps and influences SEOs and Internet marketers alike.

The following are some of the fundamental ways, by which Google Analytics ably helps you choosing a specific SEO campaign for your site:

💻 The Ideal Way to Monitor Site Visitor – Visitors is the main data you receive from the analytics. With this data, you can further receive information about your visitors—volume, behavior, location, purchasing capacity, etc.

Its importance for SEO enables you to use this data to compare visitors within the current period against another definite period, say, weekly or monthly periods. In effect, you can find out whether your visitors decreased, increased, or slightly remained the same.

Thus, it helps you modifying certain areas of your site and/or SEO campaign strategies, as necessary. At the very least, you will know whether your efforts in marketing your site, products, or services succeeded or failed.

🖥 Track Values of Referring Keywords – The referring keywords typically list down the top keywords accountable for delivering visitors to your site. Moreover, you can track which of your keywords are the most and least responsible for giving your site their corresponding volumes of traffic.

Its importance in SEO gives you the understanding of how you ranked in the search results using such keywords. Thus, based on your keyword tracking data report, you can decide whether it entails urgencies of modifying your keywords or not. Alternatively, you may also decide upon focusing on specific keywords and capitalizing on their potentials.

🖥 Recognize the Domains or Web Sites that Deliver Traffic to Your Site – Referrers provide you insights about the sources of your traffic. This becomes a good opportunity for you to build goodwill to other sites and share useful information with each other.

Its importance in SEO helps you understanding the sites where you must have your presence. In effect, this leads you ultimately towards crucial decisions for your link building strategies.

⌨ Click Path – This important metric, which provides you a clearer grasp of how user-friendly are your site interface and design. It also helps you decide how your visitors will exit from your site or where shall they stay.

Its importance in SEO allows you refining or polishing your site and interface navigation, including maximizing the conversions in your site.

Apart from all these, Google Analytics supports better Internet marketers and all other website owners through the provisions of several other useful data and information about a website. Eventually, this allows you to make the proper steps and decisions towards your goal of fulfilling successful SEO campaigns and strategies for your site.

While data is significant, the proper data is essential. It has been becoming more convenient and letting us feel overwhelmed when there are growing volumes of data collected. Having an understanding of what is important to your site or business, is a great help towards evaluating what data matters, or should be accountable.

"The goal is to turn data into information, and information into insight."

— **Cara Carleton "Carly" Fiorina**, Former CEO of Hewlett-Packard

CHAPTER 7 – SEO IN SOCIAL MEDIA NETWORKS FOR MAXIMUM EXPOSURES

"SEO is to attract attention. Social media is to keep it!"
— **Stoney deGeyter**

While SEO has been changing constantly with the evolutions of Google algorithm updates, the biggest effect of all these changes is the significance of social media for determining search engine rankings.

SEO is no longer purely technical. It has now already demanded much more than knowing where to position your keywords in your URL, meta-description, and heading. At present, quality content and social media are both playing vital roles in attaining higher rankings in the search engine.

SEO is all about growing organically; meaning, working upon each of what constitutes an integral part of a whole. Hence, when developing an organic marketing plan to be feasible, it would be important and necessary to know how SEO, digital content marketing, and social media collaborate.

Almost all have a social media account— either on Facebook or on Twitter, Google+ or Pinterest. Apart from being social and enjoying the fun they offer, your social media accounts can positively influence your SEO practices. Your gains are either direct (where more people may find your profile, connect with you, and visit your site) or indirect (where your social media account becomes an added link pointing to your website).

In addition, remember that each social media platform has its own internal and exclusive search engine (as in Facebook Graph Search), which derive search results from the information you provided in your profile.

Therefore, if you have an interesting and well-defined profile, expect more people finding you as they search within these social media platforms.

IMPACT, RELEVANCE, AND IMPORTANCE OF SOCIAL MEDIA TO SEO

SEO professionals recently urged digital marketers never to discount the impact of social media on SEO too quickly. For everybody's information, SEO professionals bear the novel perception that social media is now the new SEO.

Adapting to the new perception of SEO professionals and learning why several marketers integrate social media into their SEO strategies, here are a few essential points you should understand about how social media affects SEO 2017|2018 and in the years to come.

🖥 Social Media Influence Boosting Your Rankings – Engaging in social media gives you the opportunities of marking up the credibility and value of your contents. Social media is an ideal platform for establishing and growing your influence, authority, credibility, and value in your industry or your specific business niche.

However, once social media signals relating to the authority of a profile are all out and spread across publicly, or when a posted blog goes viral, the questions that usually arise are:

Does Google regard links published on social media accounts as credible back-links? Would these new links boost the search ranking of the blog post?

When posting relevant contents that reach to, and resonate with your targeted audience, search engines will be taking notice immediately.

Links to your contents on social media platforms such as, Facebook, YouTube, LinkedIn, Twitter, Google+, and others, practically assist the search engines on understanding what sites are more credible to merit higher rankings for what keywords or key phrases used.

In fact, Google declared that it incorporates how many times a link undergoes sharing or tweeting into their search rank algorithms. Actually, Google is crawling social media websites for data and information in the same manner that it would any other websites.

If Google can establish that you are an authority and a credible source in your contents' niche, then Google will certainly look into accommodating your social media signals and consider ranking your site higher.

Moreover, Bing avers that it definitely considers looking at this data, including the authority of the social media account owners sharing the link.

Several marketers now believe that links to your site coming from social media accounts actually have a great impact on your site rankings. Nowadays, links are mainly attainable by way of creating and developing original and quality contents and sharing across social media networks.

This leads us then to think that although the authority of a social media account does not really influence search rankings, published links on social media will most likely be marked as credible back-links, and thus, influence the rankings of a certain web page.

🖥 Social Sharing Produces More Links for Your Site – Among the many benefits of social media is having increased opportunities for receiving and sharing links.

The dynamics and activities in social media oftentimes lead to a heightened awareness of site contents. In turn, such awareness results to increased familiarity and more users linking to your website.

Thus, these social media links become great means for boosting your chances of landing in the primary SERPs. Working well with SEO and social media will certainly provide your site with the necessary links to increase your search engine rankings.

🖥 Social Media Profiles Land Easily in the SERPs – Although social media shares may only bear probabilities of influencing the position of a webpage in the search listings, your social media profiles will definitely affect the listings in the search results.

In fact, social media profiles are oftentimes included the primary results of the SERPs for brand names. For example, searching for "Ford Motor Company" in Google, FoMoCo's LinkedIn, Facebook, YouTube, and Instagram profiles appeared respectively, as the 4th, 5th, 6th, and 7th in the primary rankings.

Image-13: Social Media Profiles in the Primary SERP

In addition, at the upper right-hand sidebar of the SERP, Google showed the company's summary profile information in Google+, as well as its different social media profiles.

Ford Motor Company
Automaker company

corporate.ford.com

The Ford Motor Company is an American multinational automaker headquartered in Dearborn, Michigan, a suburb of Detroit. It was founded by Henry Ford and incorporated on June 16, 1903. Wikipedia

Stock price: F (NYSE) US$12.04 +0.04 (+0.33%)
16 Nov, 4:00 PM GMT-5 - Disclaimer

Customer service: 1800 10 736 3673

Founder: Henry Ford

Founded: 16 June 1903, Dearborn, Michigan, United States

CEO: James Hackett (22 May 2017–)

Headquarters: Dearborn, Michigan, United States

Subsidiaries: Jaguar Cars, Lincoln Motor Company, MORE

Profiles

LinkedIn   YouTube   Facebook   Twitter   Google+

Image-14: Website Profile in Google+ and inclusive Social Media Profiles Shown at the Sidebar of the SERP

More often than not, when searching for a brand or company, which you only have little information about, these updated SERP features allow you going to their respective social sites in an instant.

Social media channels of particular brands and companies can really let you feel more intimate with them as opposed to their respective web pages. In social media, they usually impart you off the bat with certain ways of receiving a sense of personality about the brand or company.

Thus, if a social media account shows up at the top of the SERP, you will just as likely to click on their social account as you would be clicking on their website.

Indeed, there are no doubts that your social media profiles matter to Google, and of course, particularly to people searching for you online. A number of active social media channels can truly change to make the experience more personal, engaging and fun for all of the people, especially your customers searching or getting to learn about your brand online.

Furthermore, although many may regard Google+ as a non-essential social media channel, marketers should not disregard the fact that a brand or company's Google+ profile is actually among the first contents a searcher will be seeing, and in most likelihood, clicking on to find out further. As such, it really pays to have a social media profile with up-to-date information and engaging quality contents.

🖥 Social Media Are Venues to Growing Your Followers to Improve Rankings– Social media also gives favorable opportunities in expanding your followers and growing your connections. The volume of your followers and connections influences greatly on your rankings in the search engine.

Obviously, a business enterprise with a million followers on Twitter will be receiving greater chances to rank compared to a competitor with only a hundred followers. However, it is noteworthy that Google detects and recognizes the quality of your followers and connections. Thus, ensure growing your network of followers organically.

⌨ Social Media Channels Are Practically Search Engines in Their Own Way – Currently, people do not only go to the primary traditional search engines like Google and Bing to find out certain things and stuff. People also prefer using the primary social media channels like Facebook and Twitter to search what they are specifically looking for.

With this notion alone, it truly answers why social media is now the new SEO. You just really have to accept and understand that search engine optimization now includes the search dynamics occurring on "social media search engines." This can be functional in two ways:

❖ Firstly, when you are active on a social media account, say, Twitter, it would be completely possible that people will be discovering your company or brand's new content marketing app after they search for content distribution-related tweets on Twitter's search engine.

In a similar manner, brands attributing themselves to beautiful and high definition visuals can benefit from making them visible on Instagram by using hashtags, or on

Pinterest by categorizing properly their pins.

Image-15: The Revamped and All-New Instagram Search Engine

❖ Secondly, as mentioned earlier, if people want to check out for a brand or company, they are inclined to opening social media profiles and perform quick searches to find out natures of the brand or company's presence on each channel.

The following are some statistics that produce strong effects on just how people use intensively social media for searching:

❖ Facebook declared it has more than a couple of billion search queries each day! That is already more than half of the 3.5 billion search queries processed daily by Google.

❖ Twitter handles about 20 billion search queries per month! Comparatively, that whopping figure is 5 times more than the search queries managed by Bing!

❖ YouTube garnered more than 4 billion search queries each month. Additionally, YouTube receives more than 100 hours of uploaded video time per minute, and thereby, establishing itself as among the largest repositories of content in the Web.

Upon searching for a brand on social media platforms, it is common finding several different profiles popping up. Yet, at oftentimes, it is never clear which among the popped up profiles the real deal is. Hence, marketers must ensure that users will be finding it very easy to identify their official social media profiles.

Optimizing this profile recognition approach may denote deleting other duplicate social media accounts and/or labeling clearly each social media account with implied descriptions so that users will understand quickly what purpose these accounts serve. An example is to create separate social media accounts for the press, human resources, and general pages.

Let us now find out how you can optimize your account profiles on the following major social media platforms:

SEO AND FACEBOOK

Using the search result for "Canon," the Christian rapper, as an example will show you how it can stand out in the primary SERP despite the ambiguities and usual connotations of its name— Canon, the renowned camera, Cannon, the popular Scottish rock band, and Canon, as the encyclical laws of Christianity.

Canon - Home | Facebook
https://www.facebook.com/getthecanon/ ▾
Canon. 69735 likes · 754 talking about this. Follow Canon @getthecanon on Twitter!
www.getthecanon.com www.reflectionmusicgroup.com.

Image-16A: Search Result of Facebook Profile for Canon

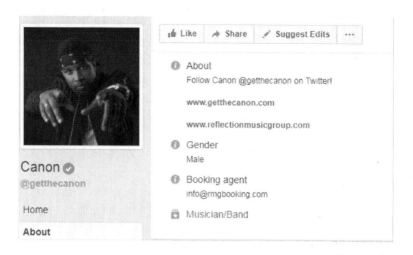

Image-16B: Facebook 'ABOUT' Information of Canon

As you would search it yourself, its Facebook profile lands right at the top of the SERP. You will see that the official (identified with a blue-circled checkmark) Facebook (FB) page name, Canon, is displayed as the title while the 'About' section in Facebook is the description.

Since we never know how Google algorithm works on this search result, we can only deduce some striking and prominent attributes that somehow make it land on top of the search rankings.

Foremost, you will notice the volume of likes and the number of people talking about Canon and its FB page. Further, perhaps, since it is an official FB page, Google regarded highly its authority and credibility. Just the same, ensure performing the following to optimize both your site and FB social media account:

💻 Optimize Filling In the Informative Fields – Fill in the 'About' field on FB within 170 characters to describe your FB account. As you will observe with Canon's, he cleverly made use of the limited range by including a link to his websites, and even his other social media account, Twitter.

You should also fill in all the other fields in the 'About' section. This is important to support your credibility and authority.

💻 Identify Properly Your Username / URL to Your Advantage – Choose the desired username for your FB page in order to have a friendly URL and not something like facebook.com/Pages/321321321.

In the example, Canon used his ambiguous and engaging ID handle, facebook.com/getthecanon/. You can modify easily the username of your FB page from the General Account Settings / Edit Page / Basic Information menu.

💻 Link Your FB Page to Your Website – Keep updating your FB page regularly by posting contents on your site or sharing interesting images or posts of others'.

💻 Build and Grow Your Fan Base – You have to accept as many fans and followers to your page. A larger following and fan base provides greater exposures to your new posts.

⌨ Install the Facebook 'Like' Button on Your Website — This will allow readers to follow your FB page and know your latest updates.

SEO AND TWITTER

Twitter is a social networking and an online news service platform, where users can post and interact with posted messages, popularly called 'tweets.' It is an excellent venue where you can also find and build your targeted fan base (i.e., people who will surely follow you since they bear interests in your niche).

Among the most common mistakes users commit with Twitter (and certainly, with all the other social media channels) is hiding their real identity just for the reason of having an account and expecting to get followers, if not, a stream of visitors to their websites.

The actual realization of returns in Twitter, or in the entire social media networks for that matter, comes from establishing trust between you and your followers or other users of the platform.

Revealing or showing your real identity and sharing valuable and engaging information are the ideal ways of building trust in social media networking.

What really matters to you is not the volume per se of people following you back, but the quality of your followers. Quality, in this perspective, means followers who are enthusiastic knowing what you have to post and share.

To attract new, quality followers is having an interestingly good description of your account plus a clear and pleasing profile photo of yourself. This is also how you can improve on building trust. Just the same, ensure performing the following to optimize both your site and Twitter social media account:

⌨ Adhere To The 2,000-Follow Limit –This Twitter rule does not allow you following over 2,000 people if your page does not even have as many followers. Hence, try keeping a balance between the total of people you are following and the number of your followers.

⌨ Be Active – Keep tweeting on a regular basis. Tweeting more regularly gives you more followers.

⌨ Do Not Limit Your Tweet Compositions To Plain Text – Twitter allows not only text tweeting but also tweeting using other media like images and videos.

⌨ Add Hashtags To Your Tweet Compositions – Hashtags stimulate increasing the engagement levels of your posts.

You only have to place the pound symbol (#) in front of your intended word or phrase (typed without spaces and non-alphanumeric characters) in your tweet so that it groups with other tweets with similar topics, and enables it to reach wider levels of engagement.

You can also use hashtags on other social platforms like Facebook, Instagram, Google+, and Pinterest. An example of a tweet having hashtags goes:

What will be the #SEO20172018bestpractices vis-à-vis the latest #searchengineupdates?

Clicking either of the two hashtags will lead you to more information about their respective topics if not, direct answers to your tweet.

More importantly, clicking on hashtags would let you discover other social media profiles with similar perspectives and intents as yours, with which you can build goodwill and further networking. Eventually, sharing useful and informative links with others will just come by easy and natural.

🖥 Make A Good Impression – Exert efforts of making a good impression and having your profile noticed by the big-name movers and influencers in your niche. Ideally, retweet their posts and/or follow them and follow their followers.

🖥 Never Do Anything To An Excessive Degree – Although it is better tweeting more frequently, refrain from posting the same messages repeatedly. Try being creative, and make your tweets useful, informative, engaging, and direct to the point.

🖥 Capitalize On the 280-Character Limit – You should take advantage of the extended character limit— from the long-standing 140 characters to twice its limit at 280 characters. Although this is yet a proposed extension announced just recently in September 2017, and still undergoing tests at present, many are now anticipating that the proposal pushes through to its fulfillment for so many reasons.

Foremost of these reasons is luring back to the fold previous users, who just feel annoyed upon creating a restrained text tweet composition.

In the light of this the newly extended character limit proposal, it is noteworthy knowing what particular contents count or not. Hashtags and links, including spaces, count towards the 280 limit while photos, videos, polls, gifs, and quote tweets do not.

Fortunately, Twitter handles (@username) no longer count. This means that tweets beginning with a username will certainly be reaching all your followers. You will no longer have to apply the "@" pattern, which users presently use in broadcasting tweets widely. If you desire a reply that your entire followers will see, you would just have to retweet it, prompting that you intended the reply for a much broader viewing.

Image-17: Tweet Composition within the 280-Character Limit under Experimental Testing

SEO 2018

As you will notice on Image-17, the entire tweet composition exceeded the 280-character limit, as prompted by the circle turning red at the lower right corner of the text box. The highlighted text portion denotes the excess characters, proving characters of hashtags truly count.

SEO AND GOOGLE+

Being an owner of a website only demands you more to use Google+. You ought to have a Google+ account even if you hate social media. You will gain several benefits having one, but the most prudent and practical reasons are:

🖥 Google Owns Google+ – Obviously, the preferred social media network of Google is its own, Google+. Hence, it is a no-brainer that Google+ has easy access to all updates and information. Since the latest impressions imply social media as fast becoming a factor for search engine ranking, it is obviously imperative for Google to apply primarily its data and updates on Google+.

At present, Facebook does not allow Google access to most of its data that will factor in the rankings. Talk about the nuances of competition here.

🖥 Receive Authorship Status from Google – If you desire to be a verified author, and having your image displayed next to your posted articles in search results, you ought to have a Google+ profile. Google authorship not only heightens the quality of your posts but also, makes the impression that you are a professional and a learned resource in your niche.

🖥 A Trend You Cannot Ignore – The SEO industry undergoes changes daily, and experts are in unison to admit that coping with the changes and staying informed is attaching you and your site with Google+.

🖥 Build and Grow Your Network – Although this intent is similar to other social media platforms, Google+ serves as a helpful tool to find and network with other like-minded individuals in your niche.

Therefore, whether or not you are convinced of these reasons, you still really have to compel yourself taking advantage of joining Google+ for your SEO 2017 | 2018 purposes. Your next step is optimizing your Google+ profile by performing the following:

🖥 Place You Best Headshot Photo – Google+ requires a profile photo showing your face. Otherwise, it will not display your social profile in search results.

🖥 Describe Best Your Niche in the Story Section –Refer to Image-18 as an example.

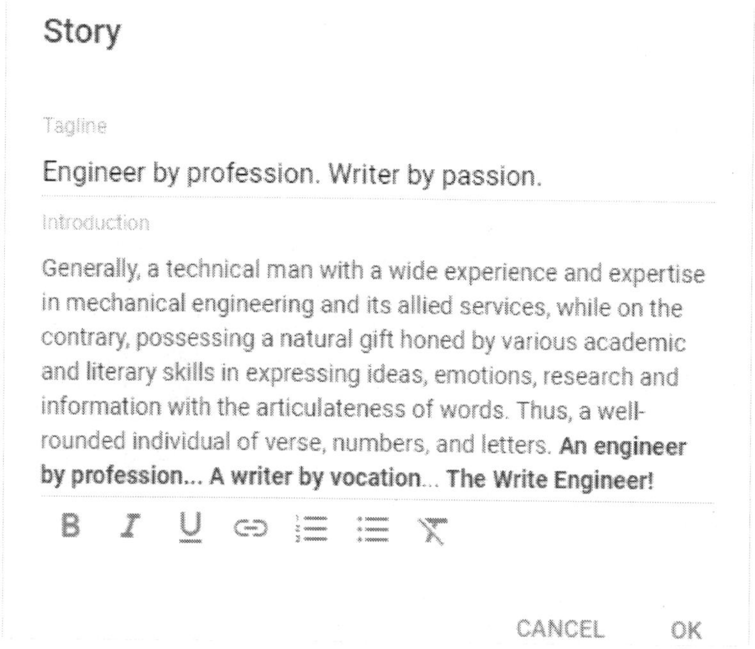

Story

Tagline

Engineer by profession. Writer by passion.

Introduction

Generally, a technical man with a wide experience and expertise in mechanical engineering and its allied services, while on the contrary, possessing a natural gift honed by various academic and literary skills in expressing ideas, emotions, research and information with the articulateness of words. Thus, a well-rounded individual of verse, numbers, and letters. **An engineer by profession... A writer by vocation... The Write Engineer!**

B *I* U ⊖ ⊟ ⊟ ⅀

CANCEL   OK

Image-18: Google+ Profile Story Section Fields

The Story section includes your tagline, which your followers can see right on your profile page. The tagline is equivalent to the meta-description tag of a website. Followers will have to click your tagline to know further about you and your niche in the Introduction field.

🖥 Provide As Many Useful Details in Your Introduction – You may also add a link(s) to your website or blog.

🖥 Add All Your Websites and Social Media Accounts in the Sites Section – Add the URLs of all your sites to maximize your exposure or business on the Web.

💻 Fill in the Contributor Section – Add the URL links to all the important websites where you contribute most of your contents.

💻 Provide Proper Details of Your Contact information – Ensure that you have verified your email address and stated correctly your real contact details.

💻 Fill in All the Other Fields in Your Profile – Ensure providing all the correct information about you to the rest of the profile fields (Work Experience, Education, etc.) in order to boost the trust and credibility of your Google+ profile.

After setting up your profile to your advantage, use your Google+ account responsibly. Ensure fulfilling the following tasks:

💻 Share interesting posts not only from contents of your websites but also, from the Web.

💻 Follow the esteemed and celebrated influencers in your niche, as well as their notable followers.

💻 Try including images and other media in your text posts.

💻 Get other people's attention by mentioning their names in your post. You just have to add "+" and type their name (i.e., +John Doe)

💻 Install the Google+ button on your website to facilitate others following you and sharing your posts.

🖥 Join 'Communities' and follow 'Collections,' and discover more users of similar inclinations and interests about your niche.

SEO AND PINTEREST

Recently, Pinterest launched 'Pinterest for Businesses.' The new concept is to provide you with solutions to your website for driving awareness, boosting your online or in-store sales, increasing traffic, and delivering whatever actions you intended.

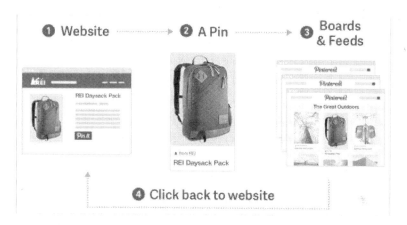

Image-19: The Pinterest Solution to Your Website

Besides being easy to use and a great source of traffic, it lets you create a Pinterest page for your site and receive a useful set of analytic reports (i.e., daily impressions, viewers, people you reached, engagements, etc.)

You can see the Pinterest analytics reports by either using the new version of Pinterest or switching from your basic account to the new Pinterest business page or creating a new business account.

 The primary step to execute on your Pinterest account is to have your website verified. It is the same procedure you perform using webmaster tools (i.e., uploading a file on your website).

Once verified, you fill in a description of your niche or business in the 'About You' field, after which, and you can then begin pinning!

Content and SEO are closely connected and cannot be considered separately from each other regardless of any platform, including Pinterest.

Thus, optimize your site with Pinterest. Do whatever it takes to ensure your pins to be easily visible, and do not forget to include a reference link back to your site in order to drive traffic.

There are several fundamental rules for using Pinterest efficiently, but here are some of the most important procedures you should undertake for optimization:

🖥 Post Your Best Profile Photo – Your photo will always be a sign of your credibility on the site.

🖥 Make a Clear, Relevant, and Engaging Business Description – Describe clearly your business when filling in the 'About' field. For more clarity, next to the name of your business, add any tagline or title you may think of that depicts clearly your site. You only have a 200-

character limit to describe your business, so take advantage of optimizing your site.

🖥 Create Boards on Topics Related to Your Site –Pinterest boards are easily visible through Search when the title of the board contains keywords. Begin following people who are followers of significant persons in your niche.

🖥 Follow the Art of Pinning – Pin images that you think will surely help inspire and amaze your followers. Besides pinning contents from your site, pin inspiring images from other sites.

Indulge in liking and re-pinning pins coming from other boards. Over time, you will certainly gain goodwill and build relationships with like-minded individuals around.

🖥 Create a Group Board and Invite Others to Join It – This is one way of collaborating with your prospects and clients on Pinterest. Invite other users not only for the sake of joining but also, to allow them pinning freely on the group board.

🖥 Upload/Post Your Pins Timely – Similar to any other social media sites, you have to test when would be the ideal time to post or upload your new pins.

Know what time of the day will have the most users online. With more users online, more can see your posts with greater chances of engagements.

🖥 Upload with Various Types of Contents – Try posting pins using different types of content such as videos from

YouTube, audios from SoundCloud, or slideshows from SlideShare.

Actually, there are volumes to speak about each of the social media networks cited, particularly, in terms of how you can take advantage of all these sites to build your brand or website, polish your content marketing strategies, or optimize your visibility and site rankings in the Web.

However, the information for this chapter would already suffice to develop strong social media profiles for purposes of SEO.

Truly, there is no reason why social media signals will not start influencing the search rankings in the near future. Therefore, smart brands must continue building their credibility and authority in principal social media channels, and should always be thinking about or considering social when designing and implementing their SEO strategies.

Furthermore, marketers should always widen the ideas of Search and SEO upon taking into account the innumerable ways of how people search contents on the Web.

It is also much prudent to think about the favorable effects that a heightened traffic volume from social media can potentially have on the search rankings, as well as the positive consequences of a social media profile displayed prominently on first-page of SERPs.

In the end, the Web is all about building and sustaining relationships, promoting the growths of readerships, expressing existential identities, and simply, sharing ideas.

All of these are inherently social, and there is no reason why SEO best practices should go against the grain of the current culture. After all, the rules governing SEO ultimately and only meant making the World Wide Web a useful and better place to enjoy.

"Integrating your online marketing efforts is all about breaking down silos and delivering amazing results. Social and SEO marketers are a big part of this."
— **Jim Yu**, CEO of the leading SEO content performance-marketing platform, BrightEdge

CHAPTER 8 – SEO AND GOOGLE'S PIGEON UPDATE: LOCAL POSITIONING

"The bar for local SEO has been raised. It is harder now because so many businesses are now doing the basics to rank. You need to rise above the basics."
— **Casey Meraz**, Founder at Juris Digital

A couple of years ago, Google issued the Pigeon Update as to how it shows local search results. Apparently, the new local search display format contributed major impacts for local search marketers in general, and for local businesses in particular.

The update was not actually a modification in the ranking factors of local search, but rather, it was a modification on how Google displays data and information of local businesses on the SERP.

The following is the summary of modifications Google has recently made to local search results:

⌨ The 2016 Google Possum Update: Reduced 3-Pack Listing – Whereas before, the local search pack in the search engine results showed seven listings, it now displays only three listings. However, the total of organic results remains unaltered.

While searchers may click on options (clicking 'More places') on finding out more results, this extra step somehow affects local businesses ranked or listed from fourth to seventh positions. Refer to Image-20A for a sample description.

Image-20A: Google's New Local Search Pack Display in the SERP (Using a Desktop Device)

🖥 Ads Taking up Space 'Above-the-Fold' (on Mobile) – The implication of a reduction (from seven to three) in local search packs in the SERP compels several businesses to increase spending on local ads to sustain consistent traffic and land on the primary SERP. Refer to Image-20B for the same search as Image-20A.

🖥 The Same Formatting for Desktop and Mobile Search Results – Although results may be the same, they still somehow differ, especially for some business types and when searching using a mobile device, where ads are prominent.

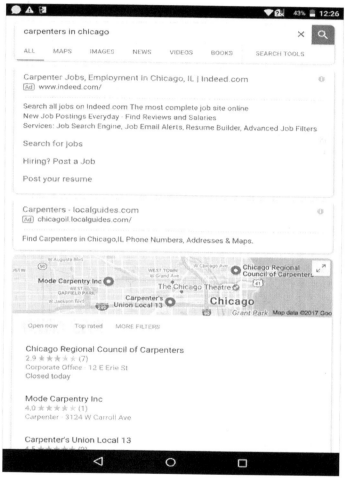

Image-20B: Google's New Local Search Pack Display in the SERP (Using a Mobile Device)

⌨ Addition of a Large Map Data – Just above the 3-pack local search display is a large map added to the respective locations of the first three search listings. SEOs just regret the valuable space taken by the map above the fold.

⌨ Removal of Contact Information – Perhaps, because of the addition of the map data, Google removed the important contact information like addresses and phone numbers from several local search results.

⌨ Removal of Photos – Google also removed photos of businesses from several searches. However, photos of entities from critical industries where local search apply most remain such as those photos of restaurants, shops, cafés, etc.

⌨ Removal of Review Stars – For most brands searched, Google no longer displays their review stars. Perhaps, there is really no need reviewing established brands and institutionalized products, leaving all the rest working for their own merit.

LOCAL SEO: A DEFINITION

Local SEO is very beneficial to marketers, being an effective means of marketing businesses online. It helps greatly many businesses to promote their products or services to local consumers, right at the exact time and place they are seeking for them. Actually, it is the ideal way of advertising your business in your particular area of operation because it costs you nothing in the first place.

Countless customers avail the services of local search daily to look for the superior and quality businesses in their locality. Of course, you can grow your chances of becoming prominently visible to these prospects by collaborating with a local SEO service provider or doing it yourself by following the <u>basic local SEO strategies</u>.

Local SEO applies an assortment of strategies for the prime purpose of letting your website ranked on search engines. The most common local SEO strategies are creating localized contents on your site, having your site rated and reviewed, and listing your business on online directories and citations— Google My Business (GMB) listing, Foursquare, Bing Places for Business, Yellowbook, and Superpages.

IMPORTANCE OF LOCAL SEO SERVICES

🖥 Local customers rely upon the Web, using either desktop or mobile, to search for local businesses. – While there are still a few people using the Yellow Pages, a growing number of people are going straight to the Web to find helpful information on local businesses for their specific and respective needs. Statistics, as shown in Image-21, supports this claim.

🖥 Local search is specifically targeted and timely. – The main reason for engaging in local search is finding a specific business. Next is finding a product or service. Several local searchers are looking for a specific name of a business, but most of them do not have a specific business in to think of when they begin their search.

Through the application of local search strategies, you can well improve the position of your business and promote your product or service to local customers soon as they will be looking for your type of business. There is no ideal time connecting with prospects than the instance they urgently need you.

SURVEYED PARAMETERS	PERCENTAGE (%)
PC owners conducting local searches	98
Google Local 3-Pack appearing in the top spot of local searches	93
People looking up a local business' location on Google Map	86
Local mobile searches resulting to an offline purchase	78
Local searches resulting to a phone call	76
People looking up and confirming the physical location of a business prior to going there for the first time	71
Local customers using search engines and directories as their primary means to search local business	64
Consumers performing local search on their smartphones, and visiting the searched business within a day	60
Local mobile searchers looking for business information (i.e., company address or phone number)	50
Total Google searches classified as local	46
Local mobile searches leading to a sale within a day	18

Image-21: Statistics Showing the Importance of Local SEO

⌨ Highest conversion rates among local advertising platforms. – Online directories show a business' or company's name, street address, phone number, and occasionally, additional information (i.e., business description or menu). However, local search directories lord over the first page of several local search results.

Local search directory marketing, which is among the basic local SEO strategies, produce higher conversion levels by up to 50% compared to other options of traditional advertising. Meaning, by having your business listed accurately on as several online directory channels as you can, you will convert a single prospect into an actual customer for every couple of leads.

⌨ Mobile Internet usage is on the rise. – Local SEO actually covers Internet access for both PC and mobile; thus, you will never miss potential customers. Nevertheless, statistics would show that an increasing number of customers on the go use mobile phones and other handheld devices in finding the best local businesses, especially in their area. In fact, the digital media time consumed through mobile all over the world is now getting higher at <u>51.3%</u> as opposed to desktop/laptop usage at 48.7%.

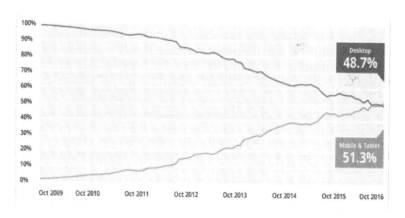

Image-22: Mobile versus Desktop Internet Engagement Worldwide as of October 2016

🖥 High return on investment (ROI) rates – Local SEO has only minimal wasted exposures unlike those incurred by traditional advertising channels such as direct mails, brochures/leaflets, local newspapers, etc.

You connect with your potential customers at the time when they need you, and not during times that they do not. This only shows that local SEO is truly cost-effective and much efficient.

🖥 Low turnover of businesses claiming a listing in Google My Business – Google My Business is a free listing directory offered to almost any type business.

Refer to image-23 for a sample of Google My Business listing. It shows on the Google SERP the name and tagline of the business, business hours, reviews and ratings, profile image, and address.

The listing also includes a free website for your business. When listed on Google My Business (which usually takes a 2-week approval and verification process), it certainly helps improve your chances of ranking up high in the local search results on Google. Obviously, Google patronizes their own.

You should take advantage of it since several local businesses have never yet figured out the significance of online marketing, with only 44% of businesses availing Google My Business listing at the end of 2016. Thus, the low turnover meant to be your early impetus to strike while the iron is hot before your business competitors become aware and getting more competitive.

Rating ▾   Hours ▾

Peter Luger Steak House
4.4 ★★★★★ (2,053) PPPP · Steak
Celebrated Brooklyn chophouse since 1837
178 Broadway
Cash only · Comfort food · Hip

Wolfgang's Steakhouse Park Avenue
4.2 ★★★★☆ (379) PPPP · Steak
Elegant destination for steak & seafood
4 Park Ave
Late-night food · Comfort food · Hip

Google My Business Listings

Del Frisco's Double Eagle Steak House
4.5 ★★★★★ (946) PPP · Steak
High-end beef & seafood in posh environs
1221 6th Ave
Opens at 5:00 PM

Image-23: Sample of Google My Business Listings

💻 Several of the ideal local SEO options are free (for now!) – Everything is free when availing your listing on either Bing Places for Business free or Google My Business, or on several other online business directories. This only implies free promotion and advertising for your business.

💻 Traditional media advertising is on a swift decline. – Currently, a mere 20% of people worldwide are acquiring their news from print or broadcast media. The declining trend continues, as recent statistics would show most dailies losing 80% of their circulation during the last 20 years.

The advent of the Internet is the main culprit for such an alarming decline as an increasing number of the world's population is turning to the Web for their local news consumption, as well as useful information about local businesses.

🖥 Word of mouth is among the principal factors for the success of several local businesses – About 88% of local consumers put high trusts to business reviews online. Hence, increase your business reputation online by requesting trusted customers to leave positive reviews about your business, and thereby attracting a slew of new customers.

🖥 Display of your business description and information – Nowadays, people rely heavily on the Internet to look for information about all sorts of products and services. If one does not find your business on local search results, you will surely miss new customers.

FUNDAMENTAL LOCAL SEO STRATEGIES

Grow your business by applying even the basic local SEO strategies. Local search trends are among the strong potentials and more significant ranking factors in the future of SEO. As a newborn update of search engines, today is the most suited time for you to capitalize on local SEO services and improve your business before other rivals catch on.

Each small business or multi-location firm — from builders to florists, brokers to janitors, or publishers to accountants— can all improve their business and earn more through local SEO. Thus, take the plunge!

Here are a few basic and upstanding local SEO strategies you can apply for SEO 2017 | 2018 to boost your business and rank higher on local search terms.

🖥 Meta-Title and -Description Tags Remain Relevant – Both meta-title and meta-description tags are your site's HTML elements, which you can tailor-fit to reflect the essence of your web page. The SERPs display the texts of your title and description tags, thus, treat this text as a form of an advertisement that you should create wisely in your favor. Refer to Image-24.

Florist in Dallas Best Flowers & Roses Arrangements Delivery   Title
https://www.mockingbirdflorist.com/ ▾
OFFICIAL SITE of Mockingbird Florist in Dallas TX 214-821-1433 for best Flower Delivery, Flowers
Dallas Florist located in Dallas Roses Arrangements Orchids   Description

Image-24: Meta-Title and –Description Tags of a Local Business

Recently, Google updated the width of the search results zone, increasing it to 600 pixels. For this reason, Google will generally accommodate title tags that are between 50 and 60 characters in length and description tags between 160 and 200 characters. Hence, construct carefully your texts so that the search results will not cut them off.

If you are not so sure about how your title and description will be appearing officially, or the number of characters you can work out optimally, you may apply a text tag emulator such as those from either SEOmofo or Yoast's Mobile Snippet Previewer. Refer to Images 25A and 25B.

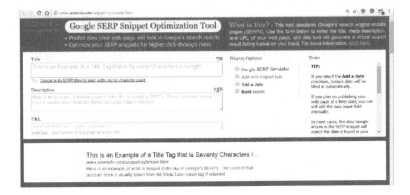

Image-25A: SEOmofo Emulator of the Google SERP Snippet Optimization Tool

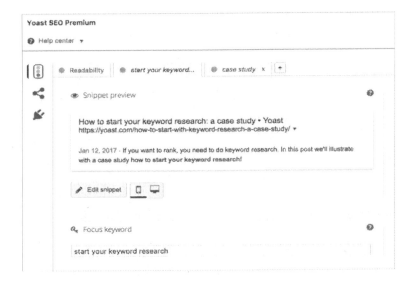

Image-25B: Mobile Snippet Previewer from Yoast

In the world of SEO, creating titles and descriptions is regarded an art. Midst the vast ocean of competing for search results, your click-through rate ultimately suffers when your texts are not descriptive, unique and engaging.

In addition, when you are not careful enough with your texts, an extra character or word is a strong reason enough to cut off your text and replace it with the dreadful ellipses (...). Refer to Image-26.

The Best 10 Electricians in Phoenix, AZ - Last Updated November ...
https://www.yelp.com › Phoenix, AZ › Home Services › Electricians ▾
Best **Electricians in Phoenix**, AZ - Simple Electric Az, Copper State Home Maintenance & Repair.
Dodge Electric, Selberg Electric, Handyman Xtreme. Turn It On ... *Careless with both*
title and description

Phoenix Electricians Today in Phoenix, AZ
www.phoenixelectricianstoday.com/ ▾
Phoenix Electricians Today is an experienced **Phoenix electrician**, providing lighting repair and replacement, electrical troubleshooting, and service panel and ...
Nice title & description, but ran kaput

25 Best Electricians - Phoenix AZ | HomeAdvisor Electrical Contractors
https://www.homeadvisor.com › Pro Ratings & Reviews › Arizona › Phoenix ▾
Prodigy Electric, LLC. 17 Verified Reviews. Mauser Electric, LLC. 60 Verified Reviews. Shamrock Electric, Inc. 4 Verified Reviews. MD Electrical Services, LLC. 9 Verified Reviews. Wahlborg Electric Company. 4 Verified Reviews. Parker & Sons - Electrical. 74 Verified Reviews. All Telecom Technologies, Inc. Mister Sparky ... *Great title, but no description*

Image-26: Sample Search Results of Carelessly Written Meta-title and Meta-Description Tags

It may not seem to be a real disaster, but it appears speaking of unprofessionalism, particularly if it shows up amidst a sentence. Thus, it causes your title or description to be less significant. Each character counts, and that, spaces are valuable. Here are a few tips to optimize your title and description tags:

❖ Avoid wasting spaces on page names that never provide useful information.

❖When you desire connecting with local customers, include the area or city where your business operates (i.e., "Multimedia and Electronic Book Publisher in Daly City").

❖ Concentrate on applying a single targeted keyword. As much as possible, position your target keyword at the beginning of the tag.

🖥 Listing In Business Directories and Citations Online – It is very important that you enlist your business correctly and consistently on the prime business directories online such as Citysearch, Merchant Circle, Yelp, and others; but more preferably, with Google My Business, for reasons discussed earlier.

Moreover, you will want seeking out other respectable and reliable local directories to list your business. Check the website of your local newspaper, or the Chamber of Commerce in your area to know whether it offers a local business directory, with which you can enlist your brand or business. Additionally, you can search for keywords as '(your area/city) directory' to look for other directories or local citation sites.

Alternatively, it is also helpful to have your business' name, address, and phone number (NAP) listed on the major citation data reference aggregators such as Factual, Acxiom, Neustar (or Localeze), and Infogroup. Just ensure listing consistently your business' NAP on as several of these citation sites and directories as possible.

Discrepancies in text abbreviations or spellings, deficiencies in the exact address, and erroneous phone numbers can create confusion. If Google is unsure identifying the correct information of your business, then it may just display your wrong data, or not display your business at all in search results.

🖥 Claiming and Optimizing Google My Business – GMB is also actually a directory, but since it is Google's baby, it deserves utmost attention and its own segment.

As mentioned previously, it is very important and useful for local businesses claiming their own Google My Business page. After all, everything is free while receiving great exposures in the SERPs, especially if you have optimized enough to deserve showing up in the top local search 3-pack.

Visit gwww.google.com/business to create, claim, and optimize your GMB page. Creating your GMB page is very easy since the interface guides you step-by-step. However, it necessitates you to undergo a verification process, whereby, Google sends you a PIN-inclusive postcard to the physical location of your business (a stated P.O. Box is prohibited).

Upon receipt, you only have to log in and input the PIN code to verify your business. Google's verification process is an absolute requisite since it wants to validate the legitimacy of your business, and that, you actually own the business. Under GMB's terms of service, it authorizes only the business owner claiming a GMB page.

If you are working for an agency or company with your services, then you may grant your agency the permission to be the administrator of your page. In this manner, you keep control of your listing whenever you terminate your ties with your agency.

Optimizing your GMB listing will be your next crucial step. Provide prudently a strong description and correct information in each field (i.e., NAP, business hours, accepted payments types, categories, etc.). Moreover, ensure uploading photos of your cover or business logo and profile, as well as images of your business, products, or services. Generally, it is highly advisable to upload a minimum of three photos.

Fill in completely each relevant section of your page to optimize fully your listing. Worry not if you are a service-oriented business without yet a location for clients to visit. You can opt to hide your physical address while you are still setting up your finalized GMB listing.

As also cited previously, Bing has a relatively local business directory page version— Bing Places for Business. Comparatively, it has the same processes as GMB. Ideally, you must also optimize the visibility of your business on Bing's local directory. Nevertheless, its directory is limited as it only accommodates businesses from a select roster of 15 countries.

🖥 Online Ratings and Reviews – Ratings and reviews are very important since they are direct resources telling you how to maintain, sustain, or improve certain aspects of your business.

A recent study shows that 70% of clients will likely leave a remark whenever requested by the business. More often than not, these remarks— either positive or negative— are regarded gospel truths by most searchers or prospects. However, you have options of using any of the several reputation marketing software and site estimation tools available online to monitor, manage, and receive proactive ratings or reviews. Among the highly recommended tools to check out are the following:

- www.getfivestars.com

- www.reputationloop.com

- www.trustpilot.com

- www.vendasta.com

In addition, www.tinytorch.com, www.hootsuite.com, and other social media platforms allow you to track and receive alerts whenever someone mentions your brand or business.

Every time somebody leaves a review about your business, whether this may be positive or negative, ensure responding to it promptly. Your response, as the business owner, will make an impression to the rest of the readers of the reviews that you care about what your clients think.

Nonetheless, you must focus more on receiving your reviews from your GMB page and the Facebook page of your business since these pages have large readerships. A positive review on your FB page can help draw in traffic and prospective clients to your business since most people rely on social media to check the impressions of their friends and family about a business.

On the other hand, receiving a favorable review on your GMB page is significant since all these reviews are showing up on Google whenever searchers look for your business. Google actually noted that receiving positive and high-quality reviews would surely boost the visibility of your business. This only indicates that reviews play a key role in factoring Google's rankings on the local 3-pack results.

🖥 Using Local Search Structured Data Markup – Optimize in terms of local search your structured data markup, also referred usually as 'schema.org markup' or 'schema markup" on your website's code.

This will give search engines more data and information about your business, particularly the products or services you offer, directions of your location, ratings, and reviews you received, etc.

Surveys indicate that a mere 31.3% of the total websites in 2016 used the enhanced structured data markups while most websites up to now are still applying the basics of the schema markup language.

Only a few know that Google actually wants website owners using advanced schema.org markups since this typical machine language helps greatly their spiders recognizing the nature of your site's content.

In fact, Google is even offering its Structured Data Testing Tool (refer to Image-27) to all site owners so everybody can implement and check properly the application of the structured data markups.

Image-27: Google's Structured Data Markup Testing Tool

Oftentimes, website owners freak out by the intimidating thoughts of coding. Google still comes to your rescue by using its Data Highlighter to simply markup contents using your mouse. (Take note though that you will need setting up your website with Google Search Console so these important tools can function.)

At this point, everything is actually just the icing on the entire local SEO cake. Implementing these entire procedures of the basic local search strategies will

SEO 2018

somehow give you an early head start with the competition; so, get all started today!

"Do not expect to rank locally unless your website deserves to and rank organically."
— **Casey Meraz**

CHAPTER 9 – SEO AND GOOGLE ADWORDS (PAID SEARCH MARKETING)

"If you build it... you may still need Google AdWords."
— **Jennifer Mesenbrink**, Editor, writer, and social media marketer

Paid search marketing associates several names, has a bunch of pretenses, and collaborates among many other indefinite terms— search engine optimization pay-per-click (PPC), search engine marketing (SEM), search engine advertising, paid for placement, sponsored listings, cost-per-impression (CPM), and cost-per-click (CPC).

That is just all to paid search before you even get involved with the services offered by the search engines themselves— AdWords by Google and Yahoo Bing Network by Microsoft. However, this chapter focuses more on Google AdWords, taking into account Google's dominance in Search.

BASICS OF PAID SEARCH MARKETING

Paid search marketing denotes that you advertise in the sponsored listings of a particular search engine, or a partner site. You will be paying either:

🖥 Every time your ad is clicked (cost-per-click); or,

🖥 Whenever your ad is displayed (cost-per-impression).

To have a clearer picture of CPC and CPM:

⌨ CPC – As an advertiser whose ad shows on the SERP, CPC means you pay the search engine for every click made by a user on your advertisement.

⌨ CPM or Cost per Thousand Impressions – As an advertiser whose ad shows on the SERP, CPM means you pay the search engine for every thousand time your advertisement shows on the SERP. (Thus, the M in CPM stands for the Roman numeral, 1,000) Users need not click-through your advertisement, but simply, it is merely about page impressions.

On one hand, CPC is excellent when applied for selling your products or offering your services. On the other hand, CPM is ideal for companies wanting to promote and raise awareness of their brand.

INTRODUCTION TO GOOGLE ADWORDS

Google AdWords is the advertising platform wholly owned by Google, Inc. It is the principal source of income for Google. AdWords offers both CPC and CPM advertisings, including site-targeted banners, and rich multimedia ads.

When availing the services of Google AdWords, you will be showing or positioning your ads on either one or both advertising networks of Google:

⌨ The Google Search Network – This ad network comprises the standard Google Search, Google Maps, Google Shopping, and its other search partners.

⌨ Google Display Network – This ad network composes of any website collaborating with Google, including Google's very own sites like YouTube, Blogger, and Gmail, and of many other websites participating in the AdWords program as publishers, like Google AdSense.

Google is only one of the more than a hundred online ad networks. All these online advertising networks perform two principal tasks:

⌨ Serve and display ads on the apps and websites of publishers. In essence, these ads help all these publishers maintaining their content free.

⌨ Offer digital marketers and site owners (from plumbers to big companies) to become advertising publishers. As publishers, they create and display ads on those apps and websites shared by the online ad networks.

Both publishers and ad network share the revenues earned from the ads. Participating in Google AdSense, publishers receive 68% while Google takes 32% of the total revenues. Think of the entire Google AdWords system functioning like a large auction site, where advertisers strive haggling and competing for the plum and available advertising prices and placements. Choosing CPC allows you setting up your bid (or the price you are willing to pay per click), either manually or automatically.

For manual bidding, you select from a menu of bid prices. For automatic bidding, Google will be choosing the bid price for you based on your budget. By availing both CPC and CPM, you can actually set your bid amount to the maximum to guarantee a priority placement in the SERPs.

IMPORTANCE OF PAID SEARCH

The most important benefit from paid search is having your company, site, brand, or service appearing at the topmost of the SERPs.

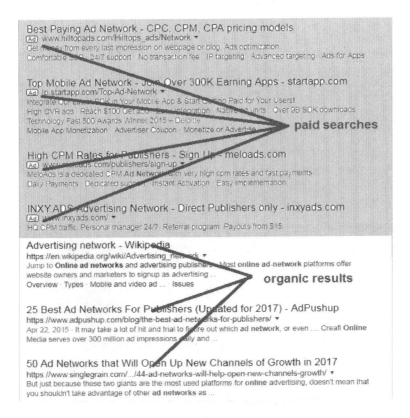

Image-28: Paid Search Displays Ads On Top of the SERP over the Organic Results

Organic results will be giving way to paid search results, decreasing quickly further down the primary page of the SERP. The significance of a site appearing within the top three in the search results stands with greater chances of receiving a click-through, and probably, a conversion.

Thus, if you have a substantive investment, pay-per-click is the quickest way to getting at the top. However, if you know the ways and byways of the AdWords platform, you can somehow set up your own PPC campaign in just a few minutes, and appear instantly in the sponsored list results.

Using search engine marketing, tracking becomes a lot easier. You will no longer be taking any risks on paying in advance your ads without knowing the measures and assessments of how weak or successful they ran.

Through SEM, you can track down every advertisement, keyword, and costs spent on your ads. Hence, it provides you with a more precise ROI. Additionally, this denotes that it would be much easier for you as an advertiser to be testing your campaigns on various parameters like time and location.

All of these, together with having the accessibility to the respective sites and platforms of the search engine's network, and having the power of scheduling and targeting ads to specific times and locations, indicate that engaging in paid search is truly an essential part of your digital marketing strategy.

However, just a word of caution, Avinash Kaushik, the Indian co-founder of Market Motive Inc. advises, *"Never let ads write checks your website can't cash."*

Just the same, you always have the alternative or prerogative of doing everything organically. If you are running a small business on a tight budget for marketing, you can still promote your brand or site profile while competing with the top guns.

Only ensure that you have an excellent product or service available, content-rich website, the proper exposure on social media, and the relevance to engage or personalize with your consumers. Fundamentally, this is plain SEO.

SEO AND GOOGLE ADWORDS: A COMPARISON

SEO and Google AdWords are the major components of search engine marketing. Both are your most valuable if not, indispensable tools when managing your digital marketing campaigns.

They bear similarities and differences, but there are really instances that you ought to apply them together or separately. Their respective uses just really depend upon your marketing plans and goals and the nature or setup of your business. Here are their fundamental comparisons so you will know when and which strategy to apply optimally:

🖥 Application and Placement – AdWords applies advertising on Google websites and other sites using Google AdSense; SEO principles apply for all search engines and show results in SERPs only.

💻 Ranking – AdWords ads shows on either the top or bottom of the sponsored list of the search results. However, there are instances when you will have the permission of choosing the position of your advertisement; SEO compels you working much harder to place in the top positions of the organic search results.

💻 Speed of Placement in the SERPs – AdWords can let you create ad campaigns almost instantly and begin receiving targeted traffic; SEO requires you a more time to consume, especially with a new website, to attain traffic and better rankings.

💻 Marketing Return of Investment (ROI) – AdWords allows for easier calculations on the ROI since you can track various aspects of your ads campaign; SEO entails more difficulties since you consider several factors in order to rank and not merely think about revenues and ads spending.

💻 Marketing Duration – AdWords traffic also stops as you cease operations of your ads campaign; SEO continues towards the long term once you start receiving traffic. You only have to maintain or boost the flow of your site traffic.

💻 Keyword Targeting –AdWords allows you targeting several keywords— most of them paid keywords— all at the same time with the help of the AdWords' Keyword Planner Tool; SEO requires focusing on only a few number of keywords for achieving the best results.

💻 Traffic – AdWords traffic is paid; SEO traffic is free.

Prudence dictates that it is a good idea to begin using Google AdWords since it is much faster. However, you should also start working at the same time with the three ideal tools for superior results— content marketing, SEO, and social media.

Content marketing helps you creating the proper content; SEO helps you optimizing your content for the search engines and receiving more traffic organically; and, social media helps you promoting your optimized content to broader sets of audience.

In conclusion, Google AdWords and SEO do not compete with each other. Rather, both are powerful tools you can readily apply to your digital marketing strategies. The bottom line is that, you avail the services of AdWords when you desire to receive traffic instantaneously; but inevitably, you need SEO for sustaining online success towards the long term.

PPC CAMPAIGN TIPS AND TECHNIQUES

Creating a successful Google AdWords campaign involves a slew of factors. You consider keywords, geographic or location targeting, copywriting your ads, landing pages, and data analysis. Sometimes, these can really be overwhelming.

Several advertisers avail Google AdWords as their primary search engine-marketing network. Nevertheless, aside from using AdWords for receiving paid traffic to your site, you can also use SEM for SEO.

Here are tips and techniques for using AdWords for SEO to help you create and run a successful SEM campaign that converts into sales. The contributions come from noted AdWords experts with their respective quoted advice:

🖥 *"My key takeaway from the rise of local based searches is that granularity is the key to a successful paid search account."*— Jeff Baum, Associate Director of Services at a PPC agency, Hanapin Marketing.

It is no doubt that the fast-rising growth of mobile search is directly proportional to the increase in local search results. Oftentimes, people search phrases like "plumbers near [location]" or "cafes near me" as a mode of finding local businesses. Thus, it is only imperative that businesses consider such user behavior when creating an AdWords campaign.

AdWords provides you choices from a geographic radius to target your campaign to a specific location. From that point, you can generate more reports on finding out other micro-entities within the particular range that perform best.

Such information includes breakdowns— by the neighborhoods, zip codes, cities, etc. to help you narrow down your intents of specificity in targeting your ads campaign.

With this data, it will form your basic outline of creating newer campaigns that will allow you to be even more specific at targeting certain locations.

🖥 *"Be analytical and creative in finding different ways to look at results that make the most sense for your particular account."*— Jacob Brown, Account Manager, Hanapin Marketing.

By default, Google AdWords provides several useful data. In fact, scanning thoroughly through all the available reports in the interface of AdWords is already more than overwhelming enough

The issue dawning upon you then is what would be the most important report to evaluate or where to put your focus first.

Foremost, you should identify your campaign objectives. For instance, which would be your preference to drive leads to your business— via web form submissions or phone calls? Alternatively, are you trying to drive visitations to your physical store or engagements in e-commerce sales?

By taking note of your objectives, you may then set up tracking down the conversions. Proper conversion tracking lets you soar with success since you will be able to correct and optimize your campaigns for maximizing your objectives.

Secondly, when analyzing the reports, never depend solely on the figures. Meaning, you should always ask yourself about the causes that resulted to any positive or negative direction in the campaign— was there any presence of new competitors; were there changes made in the account; or, were there any decrease or increase in the conversion rate.

In short, you should dwell on the roots of the issues so you can make the proper adjustments necessary to meet your goals.

📖 *"Be sure to segment your campaigns depending on the number and type of products you offer."* — Yorgo Petsas, Spanish PPC expert at Alensa, Ltd.

Usually, a common mistake businesses commit upon launching their AdWords campaigns is that they are being too comprehensive with their landing pages and ads copy. Information details in their ads copy are all-encompassing and not dwelling on the particulars

Oftentimes, they actually miss seeing the beauty of AdWords search— having the ability to know what most prospects are looking for. Thus, instead of advertising your business in a general manner, you should relate your brand, product, or service to what exactly your prospects searched and wanted. You should segment your ads campaign according to customer needs and priorities.

For instance, instead of advertising your air conditioning repair shop using similar ads for all of your keywords, you should segment your ads campaign by the make or brand and model of air conditioning units.

In this case, you will be able to match perfectly both your landing page and ad copy to the keyword most likely searched by prospects. Apparently, this results in higher click-through rates, more leads, and a growing customer base for your business.

💻 *"Always be relevant, create relevant campaigns, and give the user the answer to his query as precisely as you can."*— Marko Kvesic, Marketing Manager at an online marketing agency, GoTraffic

Your success in AdWords largely depends on consistency and relevancy. If you target your ads campaigns more specifically to the target keywords, then users will more likely click on your ads.

Nevertheless, ads are not the only ones that should be relevant. You should also ensure consistency on the information about what you offer on your landing page.

It is the aim of your ads campaign after all— it must drive prospects to your landing page; and consequently, your landing page must turn those clicks or visitors into leads and conversions.

💻 *"Creating a well-converting landing page is about presenting a sentiment that your audience will connect with. You have one page to build up enough trust to collect personal information from someone, who in most cases, have had no interaction with your brand before."*— Jillian Zacchia, Contributor at Acquisio.

Besides creating your landing page to be consistent and relevant to your ad copy, it is equally important that it must be sincere, genuine, empathic, and able to connect with your target prospects. Note that your ads only have a few seconds before users exit or click the back button! Thus, exert extra efforts for making each pixel count above the fold.

Several templates are available to help you create your landing pages. Nevertheless, these templates turn worthless; especially, when you do not tailor fit them with your brand, offerings, and prospects.

"Search marketing, and most Internet marketing, in fact, can be very threatening because there are no rules. There is no safe haven. To do it right, you need to be willing to be wrong; but search marketing done right is all about being wrong. Experimentation is the only way."
— **Mike Moran**, Digital marketing speaker, author, and consultant

CHAPTER 10 – USING UPDATED AND UPGRADED GOOGLE ALGORITHMS

"Analyzing the Google updates is the art of looking for trouble, finding it everywhere, diagnosing it incorrectly, and applying the wrong remedies."
— A spinoff from Groucho Marx's quote about politics

Google requires huge volumes of data and information to enable itself making decisions for tracking ranks in the SERP. The more users receive results that are more relevant after searching for a specific keyword, the more Google extracts and returns data that are more precise for other searchers.

At the start, in its aim of improving its ability to return those accurate answers speedily, Google started updating its many search algorithms, which, in turn, altered – at times, drastically – how it delivered relevant and accurate results to Search users.

As a search engine, the pressing concern is how to find the most relevant website pages for a certain set of search terms or keywords. Algorithms are how Google searches, ranks and returns the accurate or relevant results.

So far, Google has already issued five principal algorithm updates, namely <u>Panda</u>, <u>Penguin</u>, <u>Hummingbird</u>, <u>Pigeon</u>, and <u>Fred</u>. Amidst all these updates, Google upgraded some of these algorithms with some minor tweaks but never publicizing them; somehow, they still affect site rankings in the SERPs.

All these changes— major and minor— in the algorithms align with Google's objective and focus on improving the user experience. Google desires their search results to be sensible, and the function of their algorithms is rewarding the sites, which deliver and address what users really want, to land in the SERPs.

Nevertheless, these changes also penalized several sites with lower rankings. Mostly, these penalties were due to playing and abusing the system. Unfortunately, some penalties can go as far as banning the site.

Generally, whenever a major Google algorithm update occurs, site owners will always notice either a surge in boosting their rankings or a sudden dip in the rankings or a drastic decline in organic traffic.

Whichever may be the case, site owners are left either maintaining or improving their sites or identifying any penalty-causing points in their site for troubleshooting.

To date, each of these updates has had and keeps having a significant influence on on-page SEO practices (keyword research, targeting, etc.), search engine marketing strategies, link building, and the overall content plan of your site for achieving superior search results.

As a result, Google could now identify more precisely which sites they consider as spam, shady, and irrelevant, and which sites would likely be useful and relevant to their visitors.

GOOGLE PANDA UPDATES

The Panda update— named after Google's principal software engineer, Biswanath Panda— changed radically SEO. The update prompted all businesses relying on Google for their lead generation and sales aspects to be more attentive and be up to standard.

Google calls Panda an update since it has a search filter that runs periodically; hence, as the filter runs every time, the algorithm morphs into an entirely new essence and disposition.

In other words, some missed high-quality contents will have possibilities of bouncing back in the SERP while the Panda net catches the content pages that went scot-free during the previous update.

⌨ Panda 1.0 Update – Released in February 2011, Panda 1.0 applied the first search filter algorithm. The filter only nets quality contents, thus, screening out poor quality contents and thin websites having less SEO authority in order to restrict these low-performing and irrelevant sites from ranking higher in Google's SERPs.

Prior to Panda, any poor content could land quite highly, if not, dominate the top spot of the SERPs. Initially, the search filter aimed its focus to the vast content farms— sites employing indiscriminately several writers who turn out creating poor-quality contents using target keywords.

In the United States alone, the Panda 1.0 update affected 12% of its total sites.

The main purpose of both these unreliable site owners and writers is to rank in the erstwhile top ten results of Google's SERP. Nevertheless, this does not imply that all the other sites with multi-authors are spam or untrustworthy.

A great example is www.moz.com/blog, which has a large pool of writers, yet, enjoys keeping its ranking at the top of the search results. The site just ensures delivering contents that have much value to users.

Therefore, with Panda 1.0, a well researched, in-depth, and well-written content that also gets shared on the various social media channels continues to rank better, or even much higher than its previous position.

🖳 Panda 2.0 Update – Released in April 2011, Panda 2.0 targeted global search queries, albeit, affecting also about 2% of the national search queries in the U.S.

For its purpose, when searchers chose to view results in the English language, the Panda 2.0 filter spanned affecting international queries on google.com.au and google.co.uk, as well as those English queries in countries where the English language is not predominant (like Canada and France).

Again, the update only renewed Google's commitment to focusing to show only the highest quality contents and the most relevant and useful web pages on the Internet.

🖥 Panda 2.1|2.2|2.3 Updates – Released in the successive months of May, June, and July of 2011, respectively, these additional Panda updates only concerned minor changes in the Panda 2.0 algorithm. Essentially, these minor algorithms had incorporated extra signals and metrics just to facilitate gauging properly the quality of a website.

Web pages with low-quality contents met various sanctions and penalties, while those sites that strived and worked harder to deliver rich and engaging contents experienced a boost in their organic traffic.

Furthermore, these algorithms, especially Panda 2.3, focused greatly on the user experience. Bloggers and site owners who enhanced the navigability of their sites and published contents that engaged the users benefited largely from these modifications.

🖥 Panda 2.4|2.5 Updates – Released in August 2011, Panda 2.4 affected about 9% of the queries from users. Thus, it checked strictly on the densities of keywords used. Consequentially, the update concentrated to improve the conversion rates and engagements of websites.

To address the update, site owners have now focused on optimizing their texts for specific keywords. In addition, it gave birth to focus keyword functionality. Rather than using a focus keyword repeatedly that leads to overstuffing, you may now use synonyms of your focus keyword whenever possible since Google can already recognize and read them.

After Google released Panda 2.5 in September 2011, the company declined to share the specifics of what the update targeted, but only gave its motherhood statement about its commitment to continuously return high-quality sites to users.

Since then, Google started updating their algorithms more frequently than ever, for which series of iteration processes, known as the Panda Flux, created drastic search results movements thereafter.

⌨ Panda 3.0|3.1 Updates – Released in October 2011, Panda 3.0 rolled out the SEO-powered search filter. The update carried big websites much higher in the SERPs such as Android, and FoxNews.

It gave premium to sites bearing contents with high credibility and authority. Therefore, in conformance to this update, you should embrace these sacred rules of creating and managing your contents.

Consolidate your old website contents and keep what is valuable.

Add fresh, original, and non-duplicated contents to your site.

Place new content on every page; never re-use contents.

State only the credible and researched facts.

Have a good quality of writing (good grammar and flow).

Image-29: Sacred SEO Rules for Content Creation and Management

In November 2011, Panda 3.1, also termed, Query Encryption Update, went live. The update, however, is only minor, affecting just 1% of all the search queries.

While the figure seems so negligible, the update can be so important for any rank tracker. Considering the billions of conducted search queries worldwide every day, you can just imagine the searched in tens of millions affected daily.

🖥 Panda 4.0|4.1|4.2 Updates – Released in May 2014, Panda 4.0 became the next generation of Panda. Similar to its forerunner, Panda 1.0, the update produced a huge impact with winners and losers in the rankings.

It did not even spare the big websites that had enjoyed their previous plum positions in the top rankings. Primarily, Panda 4.0 targeted bigger websites that were dominating consistently in the primary SERPs for seed keywords.

The update only implied that when creating a site nowadays, you should write and publish quality and in-depth contents consistently. These contents must be engaging and add value to the reader (or resolve a particular issue), as well as have their availabilities on mobile devices. Otherwise, you will not interest readers but merely decrease your conversion rates.

In September 2014, Google had laid down the gauntlet once again against keyword stuffing through the Panda 4.1 update. This update had affected about 5% of all search queries worldwide.

The latest of the Panda updates, Panda 4.2, released in May 2015, never provided further details like the other Panda Flux updates.

Although there have no longer been many impactful iterations to Panda since its 4.0 version, several testimonies from sites related how they managed bouncing back to the top rankings soon after tidying up all their contents.

GOOGLE PENGUIN UPDATES

The Google Penguin updates began first in April 2012 with Penguin 1.0, and with its latest, Penguin 4.0 released in September 2016. While the Panda updates focused primarily on low quality and thin contents, the general sets of algorithms of the Penguin updates targeted the nature of incoming links.

Prior to Penguin's release, webmasters, digital content marketers, and website owners had all employed various tactics for building links. While a number of those techniques still work, the majority of the outdated link building strategies have already met their demise.

Today, Penguin applies the following factors to penalize sites:

❖ Link Schemes – building links to your website from any other sites in the Web, thereby, manipulating or inducing the search engines to rank your site

❖ Keyword Stuffing – overstuffing your web page with relevant keywords

❖ Over Optimization – creating keyword-rich anchor texts that link to your internal pages

❖ Un-naturalized Links – links appearing on your site that are completely irrelevant (usually generated when trading or buying links, where the links or anchor texts are entirely off-topic). Such exchanged links, commonly known as link wheels, manipulate the search rankings.

Essentially, the Penguin algorithm is actually a search filter that relies on Google's regular algorithm updates and penalizes spam and un-naturalized links. Simply put, its function is to find any intensive link building practices targeted at manipulating the rankings in the SERPs.

For instance, when you are building backlinks for a new site faster than usual, Google detects easily such an aggressive and intensive activity. Consequentially, Google penalizes your website, or worse, delete it altogether from their search index.

Bear in mind, whatever link you build today or in the future with the aim of boosting your rankings will possibly violate Quality Webmaster Guidelines (www.support.google.com/webmasters/).

Thus, build your links as natural as they can be. Create valuable and informative content. Raise the awareness of such content, so that people know of its existence. Allow them linking to your content since it is useful for them or they just truly want to.

However, if you pay for your link in any way, it is fundamentally advertising in nature; and as such, you should not use it to try improving your rankings.

Penguin 4.0 is now running in real-time within its central search algorithms. With its nature of performing in real-time, it only implies that this will be the last version of the series of Penguin updates.

Moreover, its real-time functioning indicates that as the search engine crawls and indexes pages, the Penguin search filter evaluates them simultaneously. It truly becomes an inclusive part of the Google search algorithm.

In addition, Google announced that the Penguin algorithm functions are now becoming more granular. Meaning, they are more web page-specific instead of focusing deeply on the entire websites per se.

This also means that the update is now devaluing spam by way of adjusting the rankings derived from spam signals, instead of manipulating the ranking of the entire site.

However, its intent of finer granularity goes through as fine as it can dissect the pages. Not only does it affect specific pages of a website, but also, it will affect certain sections or across-the-board elements of a site, while all the other pages remain unaffected and untouched.

Just like with each 'final' version in a series of updates, Google will no longer confirm further updates of Penguin. Somehow, this is sensible; since an update is a constantly continuing process, nothing is indeed apt for confirmation.

Google Hummingbird Update

To date, among the most significant improvements to the search engine algorithm is the Hummingbird, released in September 2013. The update provides Google a very accurate and fast channel, where search users can find easily what they are searching for upon typing a particular keyword in the search engine.

Instead of treating or perceiving two similar queries as entirely different entities, Google now understands much better about what their users try to imply rather than what they strictly typed verbatim.

That is to say that the design and function of the update are to improve its search results delivery for the specified keyword— yet, it is not just about the exact keyword per se, but the real intent or implication of the keyword.

In comparison, while both Panda and Penguin are continuously ongoing updates to the current search algorithm, Hummingbird is totally a new algorithm of its own. It avails of over 200 ranking factors to identify and recognize the quality scores and relevance of a certain website.

In a sense, the Hummingbird update serves as some kind of a distinguishing line between the old and the new SEO. Whereas;

OLD SEO: How will my site rank for such this query?

NEW SEO: How will my site answer best the probable queries of users?

In short, ask not what the search engine can do for your site, but ask what your site can do for the search engine's users. The focus is actually upon the users, and never on the keywords. (Unquestionably, keyword research remains to be relevant, particularly when you desire to explore a new market.)

However, when the queries necessitate producing contents that will indeed benefit or resolve certain concerns of people, you must concentrate on responding to questions. In effect, this requires you using a lot of common sense. Besides, always instill the habit of putting yourself in their shoes. Think, feel, and act like them when searching.

For SEO today and onwards, begin with the user by understanding them and their needs and wants; deliver quality contents, and then evaluate how these contents affect your page links using a website auditor.

The bottom line, keyword research will ever remain occupying the powerful throne in SEO; ONLY, its execution must align with the performances of delivering quality and useful contents.

More often than not, the Hummingbird update appreciates the application of long-tail key phrases in lieu of that seed or focus or head keywords. For the record, websites using long-tailed keywords almost always experience receiving a high volume of traffic, which usually converts to more leads, sales, and success.

GOOGLE FRED UPDATE

As of the end of the second quarter of 2017, a million questions hound Google's unconfirmed update, named FRED. According to the SEO industry bigwigs, Google keeps refusing to comment or give further details about the FRED update, except stating jokingly that all further updates will bear the name 'FRED.'

As noted remarkably by industry stalwarts on their observations and analyses about Google's FRED update vis-à-vis the affected sites, they suspected that the update seemed to target websites putting more emphasis on revenue in lieu of delivering quality contents or, implementing black hat strategies associated with aggressive monetization.

The affected sites generally characterized an overload of advertisements, low-value and thin content, and little to no added benefits for users. However, this does not indicate that all websites hit by the update were dummy sites created only for the generation of revenues from ads.

It is just that the analyzed data showed a majority of the affected sites (with traffic drops ranging from 50% to 90%) were content sites bearing huge amounts of ads. All of these sites were without any hints of resolving certain concerns of users.

In addition, several of these affected sites typically wrapped their contents around different ads, which go off clearly as spam to both users and Google.

Image-30: Sample Spam Site Hit and Penalized by FRED

As you will notice, the ads (highlighted in yellow) were the most conspicuous items on the entire page. The contents seemed thin and deceiving, providing even lesser value to users and showing vagueness on the real purposes of the site.

In its opening salvo, FRED seemed a strong tornado wreaking havoc across websites the world over, blindsiding about 47% of its site owners. FRED was direct to blame if your traffic dipped to an all-time low and left you clueless about the reasons why it had happened.

However, if you have ever learned something from these entire algorithm updates by Google, that would be about a lesser number of sites are beyond restoring if you are only willing to take the necessary and appropriate steps of tweaking or modifying and conforming to the new standards.

Basing on what the SEO analysts knew about the FRED update, the following are some of the modifications to consider when you suspected FRED took a huge toll on your site's rankings:

🖥 Rethink, Reevaluate, and Reconsider Your On-Site Ads – Although blogging is a tried and tested method of generating revenues, spamming your site visitors with a profusion of affiliate links and ads could be prejudicial and damaging to your site.

Excessive ads do not only give your site greater chances of ruining the flows of your contents, but they also depict your site as a marketing pitch instead of being a real resource or reference for your traffic. Thus, avoid sneaky and underhanded ad placements; rather, strive weaving naturally into your content any paid links.

🖥 Inspect and Evaluate Your Low-Performing Content Pages – If you have any pages that have failed badly because of FRED, you should inspect and evaluate those pages, which oftentimes, suffer from the usual symptomatic errors in their contents. To work this out, perform a comprehensive audit of your site to figure out the deficiencies and other issues of those worst performing pages.

The usual culprits for these failed pages are the overflowing of impertinent keywords, very short or badly written contents, and the deficiencies of providing visitors with potential and actual values.

Always note that Google now inclines to appreciate lengthened contents that counter thin pages without anything to offer. You can no longer afford to simply stock words on pages and look forward to the search engines to rank them.

With the advent of Fred, those ignored pages could actually be detrimental to your site over time. This is where plug-ins or any comprehensive SEO software (like Yoast) can likely be a significant game-changer. In just a quick glance, the software will quickly understand and identify the deficiencies of your pages the way Google sees them.

🖳 Never Ignore Your Mobile Traffic – Traditionally, Google appreciates or rewards websites that meet or satisfy the needs or queries of mobile traffic. Since mobile traffic has already overtaken desktop traffic, the FRED update applies to all and no more websites— either a mobile or a desktop version— are exempt from the rule. Simply put, Google only wants your site to be easily navigable for all mobile users.

Thus, for your mobile on-site design, you should consider a minimalist approach. Dump those unnecessary pop-ups and other heavily loaded images that could likely impede your site speed. Always put your mobile users in mind to have a mobile-friendly interface and great user experience.

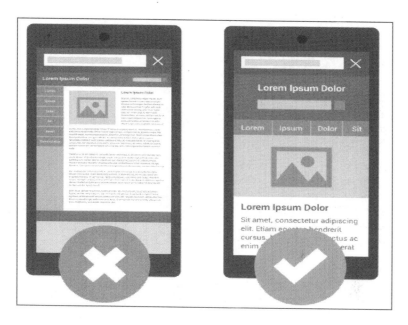

Image-31: Comparison of a Mobile On-Site Interface—Intricately Detailed (Left) and Straightforward Navigation (Right)

Focus more on an optimized navigation of your mobile site interface and a responsive design with clear and definitive calls to action.

GOOGLE PHANTOM UPGRADES: THE QUALITY UPDATES

SEO 2018

Entering into the second half of 2017, online marketers have been worrying about their site's visibility stats. A large part of their speculations pointed to the rolling out of Google's 'mobile-first index' as the main culprit. A speculative theory going around the industry stated that the search engine downgraded pages using interstitials (pop-up structures) upon loading on mobile devices.

Image-32: Sample Interstitials Making Contents Less Accessible— Left: Intrusive Popup; Center and Right: Intrusive Standalone Interstitials

Nevertheless, after probing deeper most of the affected web pages, marketers have traced a clear pattern of the downgrades leading to an upgraded version of the Google Phantom updates— Phantom V, specifically.

The reason that they pinned the visibility issues down to Phantom is the fact that this pattern occurred for the fifth time in as many Phantom updates. As an overview of

Google's history of releases of the Phantom Updates (for which Google has never confirmed them officially):

❖ Phantom I– May 2013
❖ Phantom II– May/June 2015
❖ Phantom III– November 2015
❖ Phantom IV– June/July 2016

You will notice that these updates seem to occur regularly as biennial events. Throughout all the five Phantom updates (denoted originally as 'The Quality Updates'), it is noteworthy that several of the affected pages were domains that have been notable from previous evaluations of the updates. They have become fixtures biennially among the winners and losers.

From update after update, their typical characteristics showed the fluctuating visibilities of sites with none of them experiencing a steady upward or downward trend; they just simply bounce up and down!

Basing on this data, we may, therefore, conclude that these fluctuations of visibility imply that Google is either ameliorating previous mistakes or it is not just fully satisfied with the way these updates affected the sites. At certain durations, domains carry the burden resulting from these corrections, and sometimes, suffer ruinous drops in site visibility.

So far, it has never been possible pinpointing accurately the real focus of Phantom. However, as we had just recognized the typical characteristics of this algorithmic filter, they can somehow be less intensive factors for evaluating a page since even Google has had a hard time defining it (with the implied numerous corrections it has made).

No matter, here is a brief summary of the most significant recurring observations from marketers. Perhaps, we will know how to address SEO with Phantom V:

🖥 Emphasis on online content, which requires stringent evaluations on quality

🖥 User signals play a key role in the evaluation process while their intents are a focal aspect

🖥 Updates based on the URL only affect individual web pages and/or directories, but not entire domains

🖥 Several different updates often affect the domains, but sometimes, as winners or as losers

🖥 Oftentimes, the gains or losses relate to brand keywords and/or short head keywords; big name brands are usually both the winners and losers

🖥 Seeing the results after making the necessary corrections take several weeks

Conclusively, Google Phantom V generates site visibility in rollercoaster fashion for branded name keywords and short head keywords; and certainly, it focuses primarily on those keyword facets. Of course, this depends on where a page sources its traffic.

Currently, be prepared and look forward to the next fluctuations. If it ends soon, only the Phantom knows!

"Data scientists should recall innovation oftentimes is not providing fancy algorithms, but rather value to the customer."
— **Damian Mingle**, Chief Data Scientist at Intermedix

CHAPTER 11 – SEO TROUBLESHOOTING

"SEO penalty recovery is not getting your rankings back. It is getting your site healthy enough so that it can rank again. You still have to do real SEO."
— **Adam Reimer**, Online marketing guru

Whatever manipulation performed on a website that solely aims to attain top rankings usually inclines stinking up the Web. Moreover, if your site violated one or more of Google's Quality Webmasters Guidelines, then Google sanctions correspondingly the act.

Nevertheless, no matter how upright your site is, and conforms to the highest standards of the search engine guidelines, you may still somehow find yourself clueless whether or not the core algorithm updates by Google have penalized your site.

If you are not sure about getting your site penalized or not by any of these updates, then it is advisable for you to spend time analyzing primarily your site with <u>Google Analytics and the Google Search Console</u> to address the following:

❖ Was there a decrease in organic traffic from Google compared to Yahoo or Bing?

❖ Was there a significant drop in search impressions compared to previous periods?

❖ Was there a significant drop in rankings?

SEO troubleshooting denotes technical SEO, which covers various elements of a website that comprise technical issues. In addition, technical SEO issues are more about site-wide issues than specific page problems. Troubleshooting them can truly help improving your site in its entirety instead of just fixing isolated pages.

Oftentimes, the ordinary digital content marketer would not be able to identify these site issues. In fact, marketers and site owners, especially beginners, or even intermediate SEO practitioners, need certain extents of experiences before they can unravel the roots of their site issues and fix them subsequently.

TECHNICAL SEO AUDIT CHECKLIST AND REPAIR

The following technical SEO audit checklist, albeit incomplete, is a summary of the most common and detrimental technical SEO concerns. Each issue has its corresponding troubleshooting guide, which you can perform immediately, and thereby, save you money in lost sales, or, from a worst-case scenario.

🖳 Indexation Checkup – The complicated auditing process of a technical SEO breaks down into two aspects— indexing and ranking.

The idea is that, you should observe with attention whether the pages on your site are indexing, rather than getting more confused with a 200-plus ranking factor checklist with differing priorities.

Evaluations and troubleshooting the indexations issues of your pages should accomplish the following:

❖ Perform a quick search of your site directly in Google. You will know immediately the number of pages in your site that are ranking.

❖ With the data from your search, ask yourself the following:

➢ Did the result truly comprise the exact number of pages you were expecting them to be indexing?

➢ Did you see pages in the index that you actually do not want them indexed?

➢ Do you have any missing pages in the index that you have rather wanted to rank?

❖ Try probing deeper your site so that you can check various aspects of the pages on your website, like blog posts and brand or product pages.

❖ Inspect all subdomains to ensure whether they are indexing or not.

❖ Inspect previous versions of your website whether there were any cases of mistaken indexations rather than redirections.

❖ Watch out for spam whenever your website was hacked or any uncommon occurrences (such as gambling or pharmaceutical SEO site-hacking spam) by probing deeper into the search result.

❖ Find out precisely what factors could be resulting in your site indexation issues.

🖥 robots.txt file – A mere "/" misconfigured in your robots.txt file is, perhaps, one of the most discrediting characters in performing SEO. Unfortunately, not everybody knows how to check and troubleshoot the robots.txt. Here are the steps to check and fix it:

❖ Proceed to yoursitename.com/robots.txt. Ensure it does not display the following text, "User-agent: * Disallow: /" as shown below:

Image-33: (Top) Sample Graphic of the robot.txt file (Below) Sample Image of the robot.txt File Appearing in the Google Index

SEU 2018

❖ Consult immediately with your site developer when you see the "Disallow: /" text. Either this could be some good reason for setting it up, or simply, a simple unintentional omission resulting from inattention.

❖ When you have a robots.txt file that is more complicated similar to several other e-commerce sites, you must evaluate it with your developer line-by-line to ensure everything is correct.

🖥 Meta-Robots 'NOINDEX' – At times, a NOINDEX configured in the meta-robots.txt can be more detrimental to your site than an improperly placed character in the robots.txt file. While the presence of a NOINDEX directive will not pull out your pages from the Google index, the command will certainly remove all your site pages with this configuration.

Generally, the setting up of the NOINDEX occurs during the early phases of a website's development. You or an attentive site developer should ensure removing the NOINDEX configuration from your live site.

However, you should also verify if that is really the case since there are certain pages that require such a configuration. To troubleshoot, follow these procedures:

❖ Perform a quick search of the NOINDEX configuration by opening and looking at the source codes of your pages. The configuration would appear as shown below.

```
<META NAME="ROBOTS" CONTENT="NOINDEX, FOLLOW">
<META NAME="ROBOTS" CONTENT="INDEX, NOFOLLOW">
<META NAME="ROBOTS" CONTENT="NOINDEX, NOFOLLOW">
```

Image-34: Sample Image of the NOINDEX Configuration in the Source Code

❖ Upon seeing such appearance of the NOINDEX, take action by changing it to "INDEX, FOLLOW" or with nothing at all depending on the directive you want the crawlers doing on your page.

❖ Ideally, use the Screaming Frog tool, which helps you scan instantly all the pages on your website.

❖ When your site constantly undergoes improvements or updates, always check the configurations in the source codes of your pages after each upgrade on your site. However, it is advisable to try scheduling your site auditing using a site auditor tool, such as the Moz Pro Site Crawl.

🖥 The Necessity of the Hypertext Transfer Protocol Secure (HTTPS) Application Protocol – What has been previously a necessity for e-commerce platforms is currently fast becoming a requisite for all websites.

Whereas Chrome formerly indicated a secured connection to a site with a green-colored padlock icon at the beginning in the address bar while labeling implicitly non-secure HTTP connections, Google declared in January 2017 that it would begin marking as non-secure any non-HTTPS site that requires users to log in their credit card info or passwords.

This declaration aligns with Google's aims to help users browse the Web under safer conditions. More importantly, the move becomes part of their long-term plans to streamline marking with a red-colored triangle icon it used for broken HTTPs all of the sites using the HTTP application protocol as non-secure

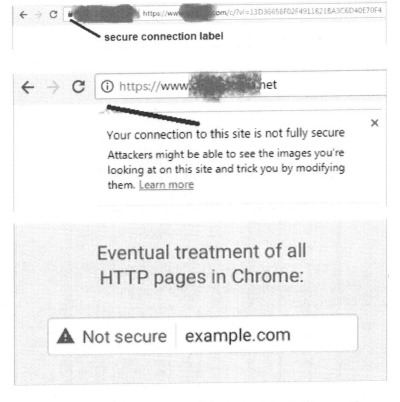

Image-35A/35B/35C: (Top) Chrome's Secure Connection Labelling, (Middle) Google's Implicit Labelling for a Non-Secure Site Connection, (Bottom) Appearance of Google's Pending Plan to Label All HTTP URLs as Non-Secure

Therefore, it is greatly possible that Google will begin providing HTTPS-sites an algorithmic ranking merit over HTTP-sites. Just the same, Google will surely begin showing warnings for non- secure sites in the SERPs before users can even click through with them. Currently, Google shows them for hacked sites, and thus, such a precedent has already set this tone.

Indeed, this development goes beyond mere SEO since this overlaps to great extents with conversion rate optimization, IT, and web development.

❖ If your website presently deploys HTTPS, then run a scan to check how its pages are resolving.

❖ Ensure that all of your web pages are resolving to the HTTPS version of your site.

❖ If your website is not yet under the HTTPS protocol, then you should now begin to plan and arrange in detail the transition to HTTPS.

🖳 URL Canonicalization – Normally, most users do not really mind whether your home page appears as any of these following URLs:

➢ www.yoursite.com
➢ yoursite.com
➢ www.yoursite.com/home.html
➢ yoursite.com/home.html

Nevertheless, the search engines care much about this. Oftentimes, such URL configurations can weaken or corrupt your link equity, and thus, make your work much harder.

Generally, Google decides on its own which among your multiple URL versions it will index; yet at times, it will somehow be indexing the combined versions of your URLs— or the process of URL canonicalization— that certainly results to further confusion and complexities.

Canonicalization refers to loadable individual web pages from multiple URLs. This becomes an issue because when several pages with different URLs have similar contents, the links intended going to the same page would split up among the URLs.

This indicates that it splits up the notability of the pages. To troubleshoot the problem, take the following steps:

❖ In your browser, enter manually all the URL versions of your website's homepage. Check whether each version resolves to the same URL.

❖ Inspect also the coding of your URL versions whether they are under either the HTTP or HTTPS application protocol. Ensure that only a single type of protocol should exist.

❖ If your URL versions apply both protocols, then you should work it out (with the help of your developer) to repair this by setting up 301 redirects of your URLs.

❖ When figuring out which URL versions of your web pages are really indexing, use the operator, "site:" in Google search.

❖ You can also scan your entire website immediately by using the Screaming Frog tool to search faster all the URL versions of your pages.

❖ You should schedule monitoring your URL canonicalization on a periodical (weekly or monthly) basis.

🖥 Rel = Canonical Tags – This closely relates to the aforementioned URL canonicalization. However, the difference is that its application is resolving the same page version with a slight difference in the URL.

In addition, it is helpful in avoiding page duplication when you are having the same content across different pages that oftentimes become a problem with managing categories and filters, especially with e-commerce sites.

Showing you the best example of applying the rel=canonical URL properly is how the e-commerce platform, Shopify, uses them to manage their product URLs when relating to categories. Since a specific product belongs to multiple categories, it implies that the product has as many web addresses as there are categories, for which the product belongs.

For instance, take the Gilchrist Watch Company, which is on Shopify. From its navigation menu, and choosing the Mesh Chrono, it directs the user to the page, https://www.gwcwatches.com/products/mesh-chrono-2.

Upon viewing its page source to find the rel=canonical tag, you will see its configuration pointing to the main URL— the default setting for all Shopify sites:

```
78    <!-- Stylesheets for Parallax 2.4 -->
79    <link href="//cdn.shopify.com/s/files/1/0686/7811/t/16/assets/styles.scss.css?30715080;
80    <link rel="shortcut icon" type="image/x-icon" href="//cdn.shopify.com/s/files/1/0686/78
81    <link rel="canonical" href="https://www.gwcwatches.com/products/mesh-chrono-2" />
82
```

Image-35: Sample rel=canonical Tag Configuration

Actually, each CMS and e-commerce platform has their default setting of how they manage and apply the rel=canonical tag. Thus, you must definitely view the specifics for yours.

❖ Inspect significant pages to see if they are applying the rel=canonical tags.

❖ Use the Screaming Frog tool to scan the entire URLs on your website, and identify any presence of page duplicity issues that can be resolved by applying a rel=canonical tag. Ensure that they are resolving to the rel=canonical tags.

🖥 Texts or Contents behind Images – Several sites hide significant content behind images. The idea is to allow the search engine reading them to rank.

Although Google technology can somehow grasp texts in images, or even extract contents from images as ran by some tests, both would not be as sophisticated as we all hope in 2018 and the coming year(s). Furthermore, Google engineers confirmed that Google's crawler is unlikely to recognize texts clearly in an image.

For this reason, the search engine does not actually extract contents from images just to use them for search queries, much less, for ranking or scaling queries. Thus, it is rather an ideal SEO practice not to embed any important text in an image.

Moreover, while H1 tags are no longer as significant as they previously were, it is still a best practice for on-site SEO to display them prominently. Their importance, especially for e-commerce sites having several pages, is enabling them to rank realistically their category pages or products with a mere headline with a target keyword and a string of text.

❖ Inspect the most significant pages on your website, and see whether you are hiding some important texts behind your images.

❖ Alternatively, for huge sites, use the Screaming Frog tool to see all the pages on your website. Find out if H1 and H2 tags are on the pages of your site. Moreover, check the word count that indicates their presence.

❖ Impose a guideline for your site developer and content managers to follow the best SEO practices for not hiding any texts behind images.

❖ Work together with your site designer or developers to achieve the same design appearance you have had with text-embedded images; but rather, apply CSS in lieu of image overlays.

🖥 A Stream of Broken Links and Backlinks – When managed incorrectly, a website-relaunch or migration project can throw up numerous broken backlinks from other sites. This is a great chance to get link equity.

After a site migration, a number of the top pages on your website may have become 404-Not Found Error pages, and thereby, the backlinks directing to these 404 pages are, in effect, broken.

You have two great types of tools to find broken backlinks — a backlink checker (like Ahrefs, Majestic, or Moz) and the Google Search Console. Using the Search Console, inspect your top 404 pages so it prioritizes them by broken backlinks.

❖ Once determining your top pages with broken backlinks, redirect them to the best pages by creating a 301 redirect.

This is the key to retaining your site's search rankings and domain authority amidst any changes in your site's URL due for whatever reasons.

❖ Aside from dead backlinks, look also for broken links since their URLs bearing the linking site certainly mess up the link code on the user's end. Akin to broken backlinks, these are also rich sources of getting or recovering link equities.

❖ To maintain finding real-time links on your site or monitor unlinked citations, which you can reach out with for an extra link, use the Google Alerts or the Mention tool that helps you receive real-time alerts when other sites link to your competitors.

❖ Include checking your new broken links in your periodic site scanning preventive maintenance schedule.

🖥 Status Code 301 and 302 Redirects – These are helpful SEO tools when creating a site migration, merging several pages, and managing dead pages.

The 301 redirect easily takes the search engines and your visitors to a different URL instead of the one they requested initially sans typing in actually a different URL. This means that the web page has moved permanently to a new location.

SEO best practices use 301 redirects, especially when redirecting permanently the page because 302 redirects are only temporary.

Recent studies had tested and proven that the 301 redirect is the gold standard despite some declarations that the 302 redirect is more efficient at delegating authority that the 301s.

However, using 301 redirects can be tricky and confusing, particularly for beginners to SEO attempting to use them properly and for the first time. When properly used, they are lifesavers; but they can be distressful when you are clueless about them.

To strategize properly the application of 301 redirects across your entire site, a few basic pointers may help:

❖ You should not always use them for all 404 -Not Found Error pages.

❖ You should rather use them on the rel=canonical tags, or pages receiving traffic or links; but again, not at all times. Ideally, only use them with the aim of minimizing your redirects list.

❖ You should never redirect all the aging URLs from your former site to your new home page lest you really have a good reason redirecting them.

❖ When your site uses 302 redirects for permanent redirects, you should modify these into 301s.

❖ Review all the implemented redirects from your last website migration or redesign for certain errors.

❖ Include checking your redirects in your periodic site scanning preventive maintenance schedule.

🖥 Meta Refresh Redirects – These are actually redirects occurring on the side of the clients as opposed to the side of the server. It refreshes automatically the current page frame after a definite time interval.

While the page refreshes, it entails possibilities of instructing the browser to fetch a similar URL by way of including the fetched URL in setting the content parameter and the time interval to one. Typically, meta-refreshing can indicate another style of redirecting URLs. However, both SEO professionals and Google do not recommend using these redirects.

Most brand new sites migrating from its old channel use these meta-refresh redirects, and it is highly advisable that they must turn them off, and rather use the normal 301 redirects in their place.

```
Place inside <head> to refresh page after 5 seconds:

  <meta http-equiv="refresh" content="5">

Redirect to http://example.com/ after 5 seconds:

  <meta http-equiv="refresh" content="5; url=http://example.com/">

Redirect to http://example.com/ immediately:

  <meta http-equiv="refresh" content="0; url=http://example.com/">
```

Image-36: Examples of the Proper Implementation of Replacing Meta-Refresh Redirects with 301 Redirects

❖ Inspect your web pages individually for any meta-refresh redirects by using the Redirect Path Checker in the Chrome extension.

❖ For large sites, check them out using the Screaming Frog tool or any other site crawler.

❖ Always use the 301 redirect as your standard for redirecting pages.

❖ Include checking the type of redirects used in your periodic site scanning preventive maintenance schedule.

⌨ eXtensible Markup Language (XML) Sitemaps –
Oftentimes, <u>XML sitemaps</u> affect huge and complex sites
that usually necessitate providing extra directions to
Google crawlers.

As stated in the Help Guide of Google's Search Console,
the usefulness and purpose of XML sitemaps are definitely
clear. When you link properly your pages, Google crawlers
can discover generally most elements of your website.

More importantly, the XML sitemap improves the crawling
process of your site, especially if your site satisfies any of
the three following parameters:

➤ Your site is truly massive.

➤ Your site contains a huge archive of isolated content
pages, which are unlinked to each other.

➤ You have a newly built site, which has only a small
number of external links to it.

Oftentimes, the biggest issues encountered with XML
sitemaps while working on your site are the following:

➤ You have not created any XML sitemaps in the first
place; or, if you have created them, you did not include
the location of your XML sitemaps in the robots.txt file.

➤ You allowed the existence of multiple versions of your
XML sitemaps, as well as their older versions.

➤ You did not keep Google Search Console updated with your most recent copies of the XML sitemaps.

➤ You are not using XML sitemap indexes for huge scale sites.

To amend these most common problems with XML sitemaps, take the following troubleshooting steps:

❖ Review each of the aforementioned lists to ensure that you do not violate any of these issues.

❖ Check frequently the total of URLs indexed by your XML sitemaps and their submission within Google Search Console so you can estimate the qualities of your URLs and sitemap.

❖ When your website grows bigger and becomes more complex, probe for ways to apply sitemap indexes and XML sitemaps to your favor since Google confines every sitemap to 10MB and 50,000 URLs

🖥 Abnormal Word Count and Page Size – You might have already come across a site with most of its pages having only less than a few hundred words. Yet, upon running a site scan using the Screaming Frog tool, you will be surprised that the site displayed almost every page containing several thousands of words.

It may be illogical at first. However, when you look at the site's source code, you will somehow see some texts of the Terms and Conditions, which were actually meant displayed on a single page, yet, embedded on each page of the website having a CSS style, "Display: none;".

Actually, this enables slowing down your page's load speed. Moreover, it will most likely lead to certain penalty issues, especially when perceived as a process of intentional cloaking.

Apart from an unnatural word count, possibilities of other source code bloating occur like an inline CSS and JavaScript. While repairing these issues actually falls under the realm of your site developer, you must also be proactive towards identifying these sorts of issues. To fix these problems, perform the following steps:

❖ Run a scan to your site, and evaluate comparing page size and computed word count against your expectation.

❖ Check the source code of your web pages, and work on the areas to reduce the bloating.

❖ Make sure there are no hidden texts that may trigger algorithmic penalties. From a site developer's standpoint, there might be some good reasons for the presence of hidden texts in the source code. However, this can jeopardize site speed, as well as other SEO problems if not repaired.

❖ Check periodically the word count and page size across your site's entire URLs to monitor any issues.

⌨ Website Speed – Speed always plays a vital role in your site. Any issues concerning this aspect somehow fall under the scope of technical SEO.

Even Google stated clearly that the site speed has always been a part of their algorithms to factor out in the search rankings. It actually applies an array of sources to identify the speed of a certain website relative to other websites.

Nonetheless, as mobile search is fast becoming to be as significant as desktop search, and as Google puts more focus on mobile friendliness and speed to augment user experience, site speed is one SEO aspect you can no longer ignore in the coming years. Thus, making your site faster would certainly be among the ideal technical SEO strategies to work right now.

Despite this apparent SEO guideline, and the obvious conversion rate optimization (CRO) and user experience benefit it brings, site speed is at the lower rungs of the priority ladder for several website managers.
To help you determining and repairing your site speed issues, here are your guiding procedures:

❖ By using the Moz Pro Site Crawl tool, you can audit your site and page speed so you can outline the site elements that require improvements to be as fast as it can be.

❖ Lest you are running a smaller site, you should collaborate with your site developer on enhancing your site speed. As much as possible, invest a portion of your resources towards emphasizing site speed.

⌨ Structure of Internal Links – This can contribute affecting the ability of the search spiders to crawl your site. However, the urgency of fixing your internal linking structure really depends upon the size of your site.

If you are operating a simple site based upon a standard site system as WordPress, the troubleshooting urgency would not be as much significant compared to optimizing a huge site having multiple isolated pages.

Therefore, when creating the internal linking plan of your site, consider the following factors:

➢ Creation of a scalable internal linking structure with plugins

➢ Application of optimized anchor texts

➢ Relation of internal linking to the navigational interface of your main site

The following image demonstrates how various pages on a certain site may connect to each other via both internal links and navigational site links.

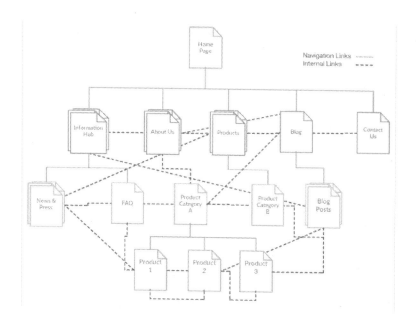

Image-37: Sitemap— Internal Linking and Navigational Linking Structure of a Fictional Site

❖ Perform a quick manual test on how you can navigate around your site. Click on those editorial-type links on your contents or blog posts, product or brand pages, and other significant pages. Take note of where you can figure out chances of building links.

❖ By using the Moz Pro Site Crawl tool, you can audit your site in order to organize your site pages by the number of internal links. Check whether your most significant pages receive a sufficient count of internal links.

❖ Whether you have created the perfect architecture for your site or not, you will always have more chances of building internal link flows. Hence, always bear in mind

SEO 2018

internal linking when creating your new pages. In the end, it can help push your site higher up in the search rankings.

May this chapter help clarify some of the most significant technical SEO problems, which are probably damaging your site at present and how to begin troubleshooting them.

For those having a first time experience looking at, and working on these technical aspects, many of these are actually easy repair jobs that will surely have a largely positive impact on your website.

"Google has become more aggressive at policing web spam, making it more difficult for offenders to recover from penalties"
— **Randy Fishkin**, CEO, and Co-Founder of SEOmoz

Chapter 12 – SEO Checklist Summary: Google's 200+ Ranking Factors

"Trust is the foremost SEO ranking factor. Earn trust from your visitors (through providing great content) and search engines will follow suit. Establish yourself as an expert— create excellent content that people will want to link to and share. Keep a long-term focus; tricks and shortcuts are not the way to earn trust."
— **Matt McGee**, Former editor-in-chief at Search Engine Land, Marketing Land, and MarTech Today

For your information, Google applies about a couple of hundreds ranking factors in their upgraded algorithms. Most of these are established ranking factors; some have become controversial, while others are plain speculations from the nerdy world of SEO.

This list of ranking factors remains to be growing, and as such, changing over time. With the rapidly evolving nature of Google's algorithms, some of these ranking factors will become outdated while others will remain relevant to the changing times.

Domain Factors

1) Age of Domain (Google declared that the difference in age between a domain that is half a year old and a year old is actually never that wide at all; in short, Google implies using domain age, but it would seem insignificant in a level playing field)

2) Country in Top-Level Domain (TLD) Extension (while the site ranks in the particular country of the TLD, it does not rank globally)

3) Penalized Website Owner Identified from WhoIs Domain Name Authority (Google scrutinizes in detail all the other sites of the penalized owner)

4) Private versus Public WhoIs Domain Lookup (turning on the WhoIs privacy protection service signifies you have something to hide)

5) Exact Match Domain (EMD)

6) Keyword Located in Subdomain Name

7) History of the Domain (sites with fickle or sudden change of ownership may incline Google to reset the history of the site, thereby, negating all the links that point to the domain)

8) Registered Duration of Domain/Valuable (Legitimate) Versus Doorway (Illegitimate) Domains

9) First Word in Domain is the Targeted Keyword

10) Keyword Appearing in the Top Level Domain

PAGE-LEVEL FACTORS

11) Useful and Quality Content

12) Domain Parking or Cyber-Squatting (registering an Internet domain name that has no association whatsoever with any services such as a website or e-mail; usually done to reserve the domain name for future purposes)

13) User-Friendly Site Layout (especially, when the main content is immediately or easily visible)

14) Age of the Page

15) Page Ranks with Usage of Other Keywords / Quantity of Other Keywords Used that Ranks a Page

16) Numerous or Excessive Outbound Links (OBL)

17) Priority of a Page in the Sitemap XML File

18) Numbered Lists and Bullets in Contents

19) Citations of References and Sources

20) Categories in the URL String

21) Keyword Located in the URL

22) WordPress Tags Relevancy (these are WordPress-specific factors)

23) Page Category Appearance

24) Permission of Human Editors (although unconfirmed, Google has already filed a patent for a site editing system, which allows human editors influencing the search results)

25) URL Page Path (pages proximate to the homepage can receive a slight boost in terms of authority)

26) URL Length

27) PageRank of Pages

28) Page Hosted by an Authoritative Domain Authority

29) HTML or Sloppy Coding Errors and World Wide Web Consortium (W3C) Validation – Lots of HTML errors or sloppy coding may be a sign of a poor quality site. While controversial, many in SEO think that WC3 validation is a weak quality signal.

30) Numerous Affiliate Links

31) Readability of the Website

32) Several Broken Links

33) Quality of Internal Links (Authoritative Links) Pointing to Page

34) Total Number of Internal Links that Point to a Page

35) Multimedia – (images/graphics, videos, audio, and other multimedia elements posted on contents)

36) Useful Supplementary Contents

37) Total Number of Outbound Links of a Page

38) Syndicated, Scraped or Copied Contents

39) Proper Grammar and Spelling

40) Theme of Outbound Links

41) Quality of Outbound Links

42) Exact Word Order of Keywords from Searchers

43) Keywords Appearing in Meta-Subheading Tags

44) Prominence of Keywords (especially when a keyword appears within the first 100-word count of the contents)

45) History of Page Updates (frequency of page updates)

47) Freshness of Content Updates

46) Relative Importance of Content Updates (content revisions are also part of the freshness factor; removing or adding certain sections is more important than tweaking the order of a number of words in the content)

48) Optimization of Images (relays to search engines significant relevancy factors through their caption, description, title, alt text, and file name)

49) Rel=Canonical (to differentiate pages with similar contents)

50) Duplicity of Contents

51) Page Loading Speed Based on HTML Structure (HTML-source code and file size)

52) Page Loading Speed Based on Chrome (Google can also use the data of Chrome users to get a better grasp on the loading time on a page since the data takes into account content distribution network or CDN usage, server speed, and other none HTML-associated site speed factors)

53) Latent Semantic Indexing (LSI) of Keywords in Content (LSI-keywords assist search engines to extract a specific meaning from words bearing more than one definition or to discern synonyms)

54) LSI-Keywords in Meta-Title and Description Tags

55) Keyword Density

56) Length of Content

57) Most Frequently Used Word/Phrase in the Content Document is the Keyword

58) Keyword Appears in the Main Heading (H1) Tag or Second Title Tag

59) Keyword Located in the Description Tag

60) Title Tag Begins with Keyword

61) Keyword Located in the Title Tag

SITE-LEVEL FACTORS

62) Contents that Provide Unique Insights and Value

63) Contact Us Page (with appropriate details of contact information)

64) Domain Trustworthiness or Site Trust

65) Site Architecture (especially, a silo structure will help Google organize thematically the site's contents)

66) Periodic Website Updates

67) Total Number of Pages

68) Presence of Sitemap

69) Uptimes of Website (Huge downtimes due to server issues or site maintenance can lead to de-indexing)

70) Location of Server (especially important for geographic-specific searches)

71) Secure Sockets Layer (SSL) Certificate and HTTPS Protocol (Google indexes SSL certificates and use HTTPS as a signal for ranking)

72) Privacy and Terms of Service Pages (are pages that help Google know that a site is a credible and reliable member of the Internet.

73) Duplicity of Meta-Information On-Site

74) Breadcrumb Style of Navigation (a navigational interface that helps users, as well as search engines, to their orientations on a site)

75) Mobile-Optimized or Mobile-Friendly Site –

76) Site Posting YouTube Videos – (since Google owns it, you can conclude that sites posting some YouTube videos receive preferential treatment in the search results)

77) Site Navigability and Usability

78) Usage of the Google Webmaster Tools and Google Analytics

79) Site Reputation and User Reviews

BACKLINK FACTORS

80) Anchor Text with Internal Link

81) Anchor Text with Backlink

82) Excessive Placement of 301 Redirects to a Page

83) Contextual Links

84) Sponsored Links and Similar Connotations Attaching A Link (such as, "link partners" and "sponsors" devalue a link)

85) Diverse Types of Links

86) "Nofollow" Links (having a certain percentage of 'nofollow' links can demonstrate a profile with either natural or unnatural links; although Google declared that it does not follow such links, it only implies that it really does!)

87) Links to Homepage Domain

88) Links Coming From Guest Posting

89) Links Coming From Bad Neighborhoods

90) Social Shares of Linking or Referring Page

91) Links Coming From Competitors

92) Authority of Linking or Referring Domain

93) Authority of Linking or Referring Page

94) Links from .gov or .edu Top-Level Domains

95) Alt Tags for Image Links (the version of the anchor text in an image is the alt text)

96). Number of Linking Pages

97) Number of Links from Separate C-Class IPs

98) Number of Linking Root or Referring Domains

99) Age of Linking Domain Age

100) Website-wide Links (count as a single link)

101) Quality of Content Linked

102) Word Count of Content Linked – (links from a 1000-word posts with more word counts are much valuable than a links from lesser word count snippets)

103) Links Received Forum Profiles (these are links devalued by Google)

104) Number of Outbound Links (OBL) On a Page

105) TrustRank or Trustworthiness of Linking Sites (The reliability of the site linking to yours indicates how much trust passed onto your site)

106) Website Listed in an Open Directory (like the now-defunct multilingual open-content directory DMOZ)

107) Pages Supporting schema.org Micro-formats

108) Links Arising from 301 Redirects

109) User Generated Content (UGC) Links

110) Reciprocal Links or Excessive Link Exchanging

111) Website Profile with Natural Links

112) Receiving Links from Real Sites against Links from Fake Blogs (Splogs)

113) Co-Occurrences (words appearing around backlinks relate to Google the essence of the page)

114) Age of Backlinks (older links have more ranking power than newly minted backlinks.

115) Receiving Links as Wikipedia Source

116) Receiving Links from Authority Websites

117) Receiving Links from Hub (or Top Resource) Pages

118) Website with Negative Link Velocity

119) Website with Positive Link Velocity

120) Keyword in the Link Title

121) Link with Positive/Negative Text Sentiments

122) Relevancy of Page Levels – (links from a page that are closely related to the content of the page are stronger than links from a completely unrelated page)

123) Relevancy of Linking Domain (links from sites in the same niche are much significantly powerful than links coming from entirely unrelated sites)

124) Link Location on a Web Page (generally, links embedded in the content of a page are significantly stronger than links placed in the sidebar or footer)

125) Link Location in the Beginning of the Content (carries more weight than links found at the end)

126) TLD Extensions of Referring Domain – (sites receiving links from country-specific TLD extensions can rank better in that specific country)

127) Attribution of the Link Title (the text appearing upon hovering the mouse over a link)

USER INTERACTION FACTORS

128) Dwell Time (also known as, "long clicks versus short clicks," or how long people spend time staying on your page after a search)

129) Number of Comments in a Web Page

130) Google's Application of the Toolbar Data (however, it is yet unknown whatever data and information from sites Google uses preferably for ranking)

131) Chrome Bookmarks (bookmarked pages may get a boost from Google)

132) Blocked Sites

133) Repeat Site or Page Traffic (users going back repeatedly to a site or page after visiting)

134) Direct Site or Page Traffic

135) Site or Page Bounce Rate (pages or sites where people quickly exit or bounce after loading them)

136) Organic CTR for a Specific Keyword

137) Organic Click-Through Rate (CTR) for All Keywords

SPECIAL ALGORITHM RULES

138) Single Website Results for Brand Searches

139) Easter Egg Results (For instance, when searching for "Atari Breakout" in Google Image Search, the result leads you to a playable game)

140) Image Search Results From Organic Listings

141) Shopping Results in Organic SERPs

142) Preference for Big Brands

143). Google News Box (from certain keywords)

144) Local Searches (where Google oftentimes places local results from Google+ above the regular organic SERPs)

145) Transactional Business- Or Shopping-Related Searches (such as, flight searches)

146) Digital Millennium Copyright Act (DMCA) Complaints

147) Domain Diversity

148) Sites or Authors Added to Google+ Circles

149) Safe Search (switched on to filter adult contents and curse words)

150) Geographic Targeting (Google prefers ranking sites having a country-specific domain name extension and local server IP)

151) User Search History or Search Chain Influencing Search Results (for instance, when searching for 'reviews,' and subsequently, 'cameras,' Google will more probably display higher in the SERPs some camera review sites)

152) User Browsing History (sites visited frequently while signed into Google receive a boost in the SERPs)

153) Queries Deserving Freshness (Google gives a boost to new pages for certain searches)
154) Queries Deserving Diversity – (Google may include diverse words in the SERP for ambiguous keywords like 'ruby,' 'WWF,' or 'Ted')

SOCIAL MEDIA FACTORS

155) Website-wide Social Signals

156) Relevancy of Social Signals (whereby, Google can use the relevancy data from an account sharing the text and content surrounding the link)

157) Known and Verified Authorship or Online Profiles

158) Authority and Credibility of Google+ User Accounts

159) Total of +1's Received in Google+

160) Votes or Shares on Social Sharing Websites

161) Number of User Pins from Pinterest

162) Authority of Facebook User Accounts

163) Facebook Shares

164) Number of Facebook Likes

165) Authority of Twitter Users Accounts

166) Number of Twitter Tweets

BRAND FACTORS

167) Tax-Paying Business Website

168) Brick and Mortar Location (Real Businesses with Offices) on Google+ Local Data Listing

169) Number of RSS Subscribers – Considering that Google owns the popular Feed burner RSS service, it makes sense that they would look at RSS Subscriber data as a popularity/brand signal.

170) Co-Citations or Non-hyperlinked Brand Mentions

171) Brand Mentions on News and Current Events Sites

172) Legitimacy of a Social Media Account

173) Employees and Personnel Listed at LinkedIn

174) Official LinkedIn Page of a Company

175) Website Having A Twitter Profile with Followers

176) Website Having A Facebook Page and Likes

177) Searches Using the Company Brand

178) Anchor Text with a Brand Name

ON-SITE WEB SPAM FACTORS

179) Spamming of Meta-Tag (which is stuffing keywords in meta-tags)

180) Internet Provider (IP) Address Flagged as Spam

181) Excessive PageRank Sculpting (typically, by 'nofollowing' every outbound links or most of the internal links)

182) Auto-generated or Computer-generated Content

183) Affiliate Sites (especially, sites that monetize and take advantage with affiliate links)

184) Ads Placement on 'Above-the-Fold' (especially pages with several ads and without much content)

185) Hiding Affiliate Links (especially with cloaking)

186) Over-Optimization of a Web Page

187) Over-Optimization of a Website (usually, overstuffing keywords, header tags, etc.)

188) Distracting Ads or Popups

189) Sneaky Redirects

190) Linking Out to 'Bad Neighborhoods' (such as, payday loan and pharmacy sites)

191) Panda Penalty (sites having low-quality contents, especially, content farms)

OFF PAGE WEB SPAM FACTORS

192) Manual Penalty from Google

193) Having Poisoned Anchor Text, (particularly pharmacy keywords) pointing to your site signifies a hacked site or spam

194). Receiving Bulk Links from the Same Class-C Internet Provider

195) Google's Warning Notices of Unnatural Links

196) Relevancy of Linking Domain (usually, having an abnormally great amount of links coming from unrelated sites, and thereby, meriting the Penguin penalty)

197) Link Profile Having High Percentages of Low Quality Links from sources commonly applied by black hat SEO practices (such as forum profiles and blog comments and)

198) Penguin Penalty (sites having unscrupulous link building practices)

199) Abnormal and Sudden Influx of Links (usually, phony links)

200) Google Sandbox (placing your site in an isolated environment that limits temporarily its search visibility after getting a sudden influx of links)

201) Selling of Links

202) Google Dance (your site undergoes temporary drastic fluctuations in the rankings, wherein Google determines if your site is attempting to game the algorithm or not)

203) Spam Links or Temporary Link Schemes

204) Reconsideration Request (to lift a penalty)

205) Disavow Tool (for removal of algorithmic or manual penalty)

TOP TEN MOST IMPORTANT GOOGLE RANKING FACTORS

Now that you have already learned that Google applies more than 200 ranking factors for ranking websites and pages, the question is that, which among the 200 factors have the biggest influence. Alternatively, which factors will you focus on and put emphasis to attain higher rankings for your site?

⌨ Keyword at the Start of Your Meta-Title Tag – Google puts premium to keywords that begin with a title tag. For instance, you wished to rank using the keyword 'weight loss tips,' but you are in a dilemma deciding which of the two headlines would be more advantageous:

Headline No. 1 – *Weight Loss Tips: 10 Strategies for Shedding Excess Poundage*

Headline No. 2: *How to Drop 10 Pounds with These Weight Loss Tips*

Google would discern Headline No. 1 as more inclined about the topic or keyword of 'weight loss tips' compared to the second headline since the keyword begins in the title tag.

Call-To-Action: You should include your target keyword at the start of your meta-title tag.

⌨ Length of Content – SEO studies have shown that lengthy contents (usually pegged at 1,500+ word counts) significantly rank higher in the SERPs.

Call-To-Action: At the very least, write 1,500 words for your contents that you are trying to attain rankings in Google.

💻 Loading Speed Of Page – Among the few ranking factors that Google has confirmed publicly is page speed. Thus, by its confirmation alone, it is that important. After all, it has great relevance to achieving a great user experience, which is Google's objective.

Call-To-Action: You can use Google's very own PageSpeed Insights tool to evaluate and enhance easily your site's loading speed. Furthermore, you have other help options using WordPress plugins— WP Smush It and W3 Total Cache, which are both free.

💻 Keyword Positioning and Prominence – Of course, Google no longer cares much about keyword density nowadays. However, this does not imply that Google had already stopped using keywords as rank factors— it is just too far out!

Target keywords placed in strategic locations on your page would relay to Google that your page or site concerns about that keyword.

Call-To-Action: Include or place your target keyword in the following strategic locations: at the start of your title tag and URL, in the first 100-word count of your content, and in the subheadings (H2, H3, etc.) tags.

💻 Page Credibility/Authority – The quantity and quality of inbound links determine the credibility or authority of your page/site. By far, it is the most significant ranking factor that Google applies. Fact is that, lest your page is credible or authoritative, Google will never rank it.

Call-To-Action: Integrate white hat practices of link building such as Guestographics, to create and develop your page's credibility, authority, and trustworthiness.

⌨ Domain Authority – Once ranking a page, Google will also factor in your domain authority in its entirety. That is the reason why sites such as YouTube and Amazon rank for almost about everything. You may check your domain authority by using the Open Site Explorer.

Call-To-Action: Develop your domain authority by creating, and if possible, promoting quality contents. You can execute this by using the Skyscraper Technique.

⌨ Link Relevancy – As mentioned in the Page Credibility factor, the authority of a link measured by the page rank is truly important. However, Google puts more emphasis on the relevancies of links that point to your website. Fact is that Google states that relevancy is now the new page rank.

Thus, ensure that majority of your links are coming from sites that have a similar or related topic as yours. Simply put, if you are operating a site selling organic cat food, ensure you are receiving links from other pet food or pet-related websites, and not from sites about automobiles or handicrafts.

Call-To-Action: Emphasize building links from relevant, yet, authoritative and reliable sites.

💻 Dwell Time and Bounce Rate – Google watches out on how people interact with your website. It takes notice of the time duration they spend on your site (dwell time), which is extremely an important ranking factor. Equally emphasized are observations when people exit immediately from your site (bounce rate).

Call-To-Action: Create compelling, appealing, and clutter-free pages, especially in their 'above the fold' area. The more engaging and interesting your page is, the higher will be your dwell time, as well as your rankings.

💻 Responsive Site Design – Since over half of the traffic in the Web at present comes from mobile devices, Google now prefers a more responsive site design as opposed to a separate mobile site.

A mobile-friendly, super-fast loading and responsive site design will land your site in the top rankings when people search on their mobile and handheld devices.

Call-To-Action: Ensure your website loads as quickest as it can and operates under a responsive site design for the benefit of mobile users.

💻 Thin or Duplicate Content – Google always prefers ranking sites having original and robust contents. Through the years, several older sites have now accumulated outdated pages, which are often nestling in the category and archive pages. These are thin pages, if not, duplicate, or even both. Certainly, these pages can restrict your rankings.

Call-To-Action: Perform a site audit. Delete or command a 'noindex' on thin and duplicated pages in your source code.

"Search engine rankings aren't the goal. They are a trophy of a job well done."

— Stoney deGeyter

CONCLUSION

"SEO (and web marketing) will NEVER die as long as there is an Internet, and search engines to help us find what we are looking for."
— **Stoney deGeyter**

"The road to SEO success is paved with patience."
— **Stoney deGeyter**

Note from the author:
Dear friend,
Thank you for buying and reading my book!
I hope you've enjoyed it!
The opinions of my readers are very important to me.
I'd greatly appreciate if you could leave your review on Amazon.

Thank you!

Roger Burns

Made in the USA
San Bernardino, CA
04 May 2018